if...then

Architectural Speculations

Foreword . . . Stan Allen
Introduction . . . Anne Rieselbach

Fernando Romero . . . LCM
Tom Wiscombe . . . EMERGENT
Anthony Piermarini and Hansy Better Barraza . . . Studio Luz
Keith Mitnick, Mireille Roddier, Stewart Hicks . . . Mitnick Roddier Hicks
Gail Peter Borden . . . Borden Partnership
Tobias Lundquist . . . Miloby Ideasystem

Princeton Architectural Press, New York
The Architectural League of New York

Published by
Princeton Architectural Press
37 East Seventh Street
New York, New York 10003

For a free catalog of books, call 1.800.722.6657.
Visit our web site at www.papress.com.

This publication is made possible with public funds from the
New York State Council on the Arts, a State agency.

NYSCA
New York State Council on the Arts

Additional support provided by the LEF Foundation.

Editing . . . Megan Carey
Editorial assistance . . . John McGill and Lauren Nelson
Series design . . . Deb Wood
Design . . . Jan Haux

Special thanks to . . . Nettie Aljian, Nicola Bednarek, Janet Behning, Penny (Yuen Pik) Chu,
Russell Fernandez, Clare Jacobson, John King, Mark Lamster, Nancy Eklund Later, Linda
Lee, Katharine Myers, Molly Rouzie, Jane Sheinman, Scott Tennent, Jennifer Thompson, and
Joseph Weston of Princeton Architectural Press —Kevin C. Lippert, publisher

Library of Congress Cataloging-in-Publication Data
Young architects, 6. If– then : architectural speculations / foreword, Stan Allen ; introduction,
Anne Rieselbach ... [et al.].
     p. cm.
 ISBN 1-56898-512-6 (pbk. : alk. paper)
 1. Young Architects Forum. 2. Architecture—Awards—United States. 3. Architecture—
United States—21st century. 4. Young architects—United States. I. Title: Young architects
six. II. Title: If– then. III. Princeton Architectural Press. IV. Architectural League of New York.
 NA2340.Y6795 2005
 720'.92'273–dc22

                              2004023385

Contents

Acknowledgments

Rosalie Genevro

Executive Director, The Architectural League of New York

If...Then is the Architectural League's twenty-third Young Architects Forum, an annual competition, exhibition, and publication of work by architects ten years or less out of undergraduate or graduate school. Inclusive in intent, format, and content, the competition draws entrants from across North America. Winners are selected for outstanding work, built or unbuilt, as well as for clarity of intent as expressed in their response to the exhibition theme.

Each year since the program's inception, the theme has been shaped by the League's Young Architects Committee, comprised of past winners. The committee also selects leading members of the design community to serve alongside them on the competition jury. The League would like to thank 2003–04 Young Architects committee members Stella Betts, Makram el-Kadi, and Eric Liftin for their time and expertise.

The Architectural League gratefully acknowledges the support of the LEF Foundation for this publication.

The Young Architects Forum was made possible by the generous support of Artemide, Hunter Douglas Window Fashions, Dornbracht, A. E. Greyson & Company, and Tischler und Sohn. League programs are also made possible, in part, by public funds from the New York State Council on the Arts, a State agency.

Foreword

Stan Allen

Architect; Dean of the School of Architecture, Princeton University

The title of this year's Young Architects competition derives from the language of the computer program. "If...then" is the contingent phrase built into the architecture of programming. With its origins in mathematical reasoning, it is the logical gate that indicates distinct pathways through the intricate structure of the computer algorithm. As such, it signals that architecture is entering a new phase in its complex relationship to digital technology.

The definitive history of architecture's relationship to the computer has yet to be written, but it would necessarily start with technology transferred from the military and engineering disciplines in the immediate postwar period. In recent decades, as the computer's impact has shifted from the purely technical, it is possible to discern three distinct phases in architecture's ongoing efforts to come to terms with what is still an evolving technology. In the first stage, under the influence of cyberpunk and deconstruction, the engagement with digital technology was primarily metaphorical. As access to the Internet expanded in the 1980s, many architects were fascinated by the potential of networked interconnectivity and fluid personal identity promised by this emergent technology. The problem was that in reality available computer technologies were slow and expensive. Architects tried to capture some of this new sensibility through experimental projects and installations, sometimes incorporating images of new media, but these projects were for the most part realized by conventional means. It was not until the mid-1990s that new modeling software (developed in some instances for digital animation by the film industry) began to be widely available and, more importantly, taught in schools of architecture. This represents the second phase, in which the effect of digital technology is primarily formal. An interest in continuous surfaces and formal complexity characterizes the work produced in this stage. A new virtuosity emerged as architects excitedly explored the formal potential of these rapidly developing modeling tools. As visually compelling as this work could be, it was often criticized for its limited engagement with the realities of construction and for a sometimes naive relationship to actual architectural programs.

I'd like to think that we are now entering a third, more mature phase in our relationship to digital technology. Thanks in part to a new generation of architects who have been educated entirely within the digital regime, and on the other hand to the first generation of digitally trained architects who have continued to evolve their thinking, the computer is beginning to have a practical impact, beyond the formal or the metaphorical. We are now entering a stage in which digital technology is understood in terms of its strategic and operational potential. In part this is generational, and in part it is a product of the advancement of the technologies themselves. In both of the first two stages, the computer retained something of a cultlike status. It divided architecture into believers and non-believers, a world of high priests, disciples, and enthusiastic converts. Today, all that has changed. Digital technology has become democratized. Hardware and software are cheap, widely available, and user-friendly. A new generation that has grown up with digital technology has created an enormous reservoir of expertise.

None of the architects selected for the competition specifically identify themselves as "digital" architects; for this generation, the computer is not a new technology to be either celebrated or deconstructed—it is simply a fact of life. They have absorbed its logic into their own practices and habits of thought. Hence it is entirely appropriate that the work of this diverse group is assembled under the sign of the computer algorithm.

"If...then" suggests that the complexities of contemporary architectural practice cannot be effectively met either by the self-assured certainties of modernism (which in many cases turned out to be wrong-headed), or by the ironies of postmodernism (which in many cases turned out to be trivial). In a move that has little to do with the literal incorporation of digital technologies, but everything to do with a new way of thinking made possible by the penetration of networked technologies into all aspects of our everyday life, these architects suggest that what we need today are robust and flexible architectural propositions: statements that are contingent rather than definitive; propositions that recognize uncertainty and unpredictability, and that presuppose an architecture that is interactive, responsive, and adaptable.

Some of these architects are learning from the flexible algorithms of the computer and developing forms of practice that are more agile and responsive. In this case, "if...then" implies new strategies of implementation that go beyond architecture's traditional architect/client/builder relationships to position architectural practice more strategically and proactively. Building program is seen through a similar lens. Use is not stated definitively; rather, architecture is seen as an adaptive scaffold that can evolve over time, open to the contingencies of contemporary life and capable of sponsoring a variety of activities. Other architects engage the very real possibilities of digital fabrication that have emerged as a productive new design territory. In this case, the computer's effect has been extended from visualization to fabrication, with a direct impact on the making of buildings. What we could say about all of these young architects is that for them, the most important question today is not new forms, but new forms of practice.

In the end, the work has been chosen (thankfully) for quality and not for conformance to the stated theme. However, in this instance the theme captures a pervasive mindset among younger architects, and perhaps signals a larger paradigm shift. That a collection of the best work by young architects can be logically assembled under the contingent phrase "If...then" suggests that one of architecture's most urgent tasks today is to face uncertainty not with vague propositions or old models of flexibility, but with projects that are architecturally specific and programmatically indeterminate. This is evident in the formal and operational virtuosity of Tom Wiscombe (who signals his interest in information technology directly through the name of his studio, EMERGENT), as well as in the inventive programmatic strategies of Gail Peter Borden and Miloby Ideasystem. Fernando Romero, who was steeped in operational strategy at OMA, proposes to reinvent his architectural practice from the ground up. Mitnick Roddier Hicks finds overlooked potential in marginal urban sites. Studio Luz engages the new possibilities of digital fabrication, not as an end in itself but rather as "a dynamic web of alliances and oppositions." Each of these practices offers an individual take on the speculative proposition "if...then"; collectively, they sketch out a future in which new forms of architectural practice might emerge.

Introduction

Anne Rieselbach

Program Director, The Architectural League of New York

The competition theme "if...then" was developed by the Architectural League's Young Architects Committee, a group of past competition winners, in response to the League's year-long program initiative "Architecture as Catalyst." Throughout the year the League's lectures and panel discussions explored whether new architecture—as object, event, or context—can be a means for cities and institutions to reinvent themselves and revitalize their surroundings and whether the formal programming of a given building can shape or reshape its use. The committee extrapolated these ideas by looking at how architects create strategies to design structures that accommodate separate but interrelated needs. The call for entries encouraged entrants to examine the role that architecture plays in providing symbols of cultural value and spaces for cultural production for the public. The committee outlined a series of questions for entrants to consider in light of the opportunities an architect has for rethinking site, program, form, technology, and materials. The questions focused on the speculative nature of design and how, in essence, architects must construct "social fictions" that interpret social and pragmatic concerns in order to transform the raw materials of site and building program into built form.

Every architectural project begins with, as described in the call for entries, "an act of imagination...that speculates on future events in a space that does not yet exist." These architectural fictions require an informed imagination that transforms pragmatic givens such as program, site, and budget to an inspired built form—ideally, a form that accommodates present and future use while at the same time making tangible the underlying meaning for each client as well as the architect's aesthetic intent. As in prior years, entrants were asked to edit and explicate their portfolios—which could contain built, unbuilt, and theoretical projects—in a way that connected the underlying ideas of their work to the competition theme.

The competition drew over one hundred entries from across North America. In addition to committee members Stella Betts, Makram el-Kadi, and Eric Liftin, jurors were Preston Scott Cohen, Cynthia Davidson, Michael Maltzan, and Wendy Evans Joseph. Winners, who subsequently exhibited and lectured on their work at the Architectural League, were selected for the overall quality of their projects as well as for how their designs might evoke new ways of understanding and even perhaps transforming traditional concepts of program and form.

Work by the six winning firms varied widely in style, scale, and construction. They did, nevertheless, share a number of ideas. Much of the work demonstrated non-hierarchical design strategies. A certain reciprocity of relationships—embodied in the exhibition by elements such as webs, mirrors, and repetitive frames—created a cohesively linked set of parts. Networks of relationships between these similarly weighted elements—rather than a centered whole—shaped many of the installations built by the competition winners as they do their work as a whole.

Fernando Romero, principal of the Mexico City firm Laboratorio de la Ciudad de Mexico (LCM), is interested in "designing an architecture that is able to translate contemporary society." Interests, resources, and program are analyzed to create a site-specific solution. The firm faces the challenges of building in an underdeveloped economy with a low-paid labor force often bound to prevailing handcraft techniques. Some work, such as the thirty-four-story 500-Person Tower apartment building, is designed in a spare modernist vocabulary that allows for simple building methods. Others, such as the Dolls' House—a fluidly rounded extension to a rectilinear home designed in the 1950s—required a more specialized approach to construction. LCM's installation documented, digitally and graphically, the steps from design and construction to finished form.

EMERGENT, Tom Wiscombe's Los Angeles firm, is "dedicated to researching issues of globalism, technology, and materiality through built form." Their work attempts to accommodate the needs of a "dynamic networked society" with design solutions that reflect biological rather than artistic models. The resulting forms, according to Wiscombe, concentrate on "the propagating logic of landscape, infrastructure, and network rather than the dead-end logic of order, structure, and facade." MoMA/P.S.1 Urban Beach, EMERGENT's summer courtyard installation at P.S.1 in 2003, gives form to this non-hierarchical approach. Two principal elements, the "Leisure Landscape," comprised of pools and sundecks and small interconnected units which form the "Micromultiple Roof," shift and at times interlock in a dynamic relationship.

Anthony Piermarini and Hansy Better Barraza created a weblike, laser-cut armature of interlocked similar pieces of cold rolled steel to hold images of work by their Boston firm Studio Luz. Their projects, a collection of commercial and institutional work, could be examined through magnified viewers housed in frosted Plexiglas cases set within the lacy structure. Some of their work, such as the Mail-slot System for the Harvard Design School and the Diva Lounge, with its quiltlike, skylight-dome-clad walls and ceiling, were designed with a similar strategy utilizing simple elements that gain meaning through repetition. Large-scale projects, including the Leominster Assembly of God Fellowship Center, an environmentally sensitive multiuse addition to an existing structure, are designed to create an architecture with a "dialogic relationship with its users, receiving and creating meaning."

Images of work by Keith Mitnick, Mireille Roddier, and Stewart Hicks were set on a series of linked and canted wooden viewing tables, which created a strong visual spine. The firm, based in Ann Arbor, has designed a number of houses and small institutional buildings, including their Burnham Competition prize-winning entry for the Spertus Institute in Chicago. Throughout their work the firm examines "spatial and symbolic" territories: their harmonies and their discord. For the Spertus Institute this meant identifying and creating spaces for a variety of programmatic needs, equally weighting each spatial need rather than privileging one, resulting in a form that attempts to destabilize conventional readings of a monolithic institutional building. Other projects, such as the LL House in Ohio, with its irregular geometry, spatially reinterpret new cultural patterns of domesticity.

Raleigh architect Gail Peter Borden's architectural investigations were represented by drawings, models, and small sketches that tiled the gallery wall—just some of a thirty-box collection of 3 x 5 cards that document initial ideas behind each project. Borden's work primarily focuses on issues of standardization, prefabrication, seriality, and iconography in the suburban landscape. One of his designs, the Rubber-banded House, features a mutable interior wall system composed of steel cable supports tied by rubber bands. A theoretical series of "experience" pavilions, displayed in a group of self-contained box/pedestals, explored concepts such as threshold, path, corridor, and frame. Borden's experimental work fuses with pragmatic design in his series "20 Propositions for Suburban Living," a group of schemes for modular affordable housing currently being developed for construction.

A wall of mirrored Plexiglas boxes designed by Tobias Lundquist of the New York City firm Miloby Ideasystem (in partnership with Milana Kosovac) explored "the notion of context." Intended to examine the "paradox between an exhibit and to exhibit," the architects described the resulting mirrored walls as confronting viewers with the possibility of both the "camouflage" offered by the reflected surroundings and "narcissism," which mimics "self-manifestation." The intermingled readings are indicative of the firm's interest in the frequent "oscillation between interpretation and experience" that fosters the "process of finding form." A number of residential and commercial projects revisit, reconfigure, and reclad existing structures. Throughout their work, the firm's ambition is to design in a process that allows "open movement of ideas across media, scale, and disciplines," drawing on sources ranging from technology and theory to pop culture.

The Young Architects' responses to "if...then" demonstrate strategies for designing for the frequently shifting and expanding geographic, virtual, and conceptual conditions of contemporary society. Many designs innovatively explore and integrate new building technologies as a means to reinvent structure and form. In constantly finding multiple readings of "if," the designers are freed to flexibly reconfigure the resulting "then."

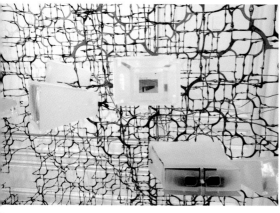

Recalibrating
Cultural
Geography

Biographies

Fernando Romero formed Laboratorio de la Ciudad de Mexico (LCM) in 1998. The firm pursues a new agenda in the practice of architecture by generating unprecedented spaces, exploring uncharted geometries, developing new materials, and applying current construction methods. He was president of the student society at the Universidad Iberoamericana in 1994 and graduated in 1995. He worked at Office of Metropolitan Architecture in Rotterdam from 1997 to 2000. Romero is currently a visiting professor at Columbia University in New York. He has received many prizes, such as the World Economic Forum's GLT (Global Leader of Tomorrow) and has produced several books, including *ZMVM, Hyper Border 2050*, and *The Air Is Blue.*

Tom Wiscombe is an architect based in Los Angeles. In 1999 he founded EMERGENT, a network of designers and technicians dedicated to researching issues of globalism, technology, and materiality through built form. The studio's work has been exhibited and published internationally and was recently featured in the Glamour show at the SFMoMA. Wiscombe maintains an active partnership with Coop Himmelb(l)au, where he has been Chief Designer and Project Partner for ten years. He is best known for his award-winning work in collaboration with principal Wolf D. Prix on the Musée des Confluences in Lyon, the BMW World in Munich, and the Akron Art Museum. Educated at UCLA (M. Arch) and UC Berkeley, Wiscombe has taught design and technology at SCI-Arc, UCLA, and the University of Applied Arts in Vienna.

Studio Luz was founded in 2002 by Hansy Better Barraza and Anthony Piermarini. Their practice embraces architecture as an agent in producing and reproducing social relationships and questions the cultural conditions of the everyday experience to inspire creativity. Both partners received their B. Arch degrees from Cornell University and their master's degrees from the Harvard Design School (Piermarini, M. Arch; Barraza, MAUD). Piermarini previously worked for Kennedy & Violich Architecture and their material research branch, MATx, in Boston. Barraza worked with the Boston firm Office dA, and is currently an assistant professor at the Rhode Island School of Design.

Keith Mitnick is Assistant Professor of Architecture at the University of Michigan, where he held the 2000–01 Sanders Fellowship in Architecture. He also taught at UC Berkeley and in 1995 began an architectural practice in the Bay Area with Mireille Roddier, who is also Assistant Professor at Michigan and received the Sanders Fellowship the following year (2001–02). Both have received numerous grants and awards, including individual Graham Foundation research grants and the BSA "Unbuilt Architecture" award. Mitnick was the recipient of the 2002 Burnham Prize Fellowship to the American Academy in Rome, and Roddier was awarded the 2000 Gabriel Prize and a residency to the Cité Internationale des Arts in Paris. Stewart Hicks is a graduate of the undergraduate program in architecture at the University of Michigan (B. Arch) and is currently pursuing his master's degree in architecture at Princeton University.

Gail Peter Borden attended Rice University for his undergraduate education, receiving degrees in fine arts, art history, and architecture, and the Harvard Design School (M. Arch). He has worked for Gensler and Associates and the Renzo Piano Building Workshop in Paris. Currently teaching at North Carolina State University's College of Design, and principal of Borden Partnership since 1998, his work has won national and international recognition, including the Watkins Traveling Fellowship, a Graham Foundation grant, AIA award recognitions, teaching awards, and an artist-in-residence at the Chinati Foundation. As an artist, theorist, and practitioner, his research and practice focus on the role of architecture in suburban culture.

Founded in 2001 by Tobias Lundquist and Milana Kosovac, the multidisciplinary studio Miloby Ideasystem has produced a body of work that spans in scope from brand identities to architecture. The firm has earned international recognition, including awards from Solutia, *Print* magazine, and *ID* magazine. A native of Sweden, Lundquist studied at the University of Stockholm, in Vienna at HAK, and earned his B. Arch from SCI-Arc. He has worked for Studio Daniel Libeskind, Solomon Cordwell Buenz and Associates, and SOM. Milana Kosovac grew up in northern Canada and received her M. Arch from Dalhousie University. She interned with Dominique Perrault, RoTo, and Frank Gehry prior to her award-winning set design work for film and television.

LCM/FERNANDO ROMERO

Laboratorio de la Ciudad de Mexico

Our office is interested in creating architecture that is both accessible and appropriate to contemporary society—a task that requires the translation of various interests, ambitions, resources, and programs. Once brought to an analytical plane, these sets of conditions can be reviewed and used to establish a clear system, enabling each project to exploit its specific context.

The office gathers specialists from different disciplines to feed and materialize each scheme. Our design process involves assembling information and experience from a broad group of engineers and consultants who remain involved in all stages. Software specialists and designers work together to guarantee solutions specific to the ambitions of each project.

Without submitting to the constraints of fixed terminology, this close attention to context results in architecture that ranges from the translation of modernism ("boxes" for which the main priorities are schedule and economy) to more dynamic design processes based on technological advances and experimentation. Ultimately, we consider humans to be evolutionary beings with the tools and skills to rethink their own modernity.

Situated in an underdeveloped economy, our office has the unique opportunity and challenge of maintaining participation in the international discourse while exploiting the virtues of our national context—a cheap labor force, the prevalence of handcraft technique, and fresh implementations of recycled technology.

DOLLS' HOUSE

Mexico City, 2000–01

This project for a room in Desierto de los Leones presented LCM with a great opportunity to experiment with design process and new construction systems. The concept is that one continuous skin wraps over and into itself, defining the interior space and creating a ramp linking it to the garden in which it sits.

The volume generated was envisioned as the confrontation of two distinct moments in history: a contemporary outgrowth of a 1950s modernist house in Mexico City, built to accommodate the family's expansion requirements (a children's playroom). The room was constructed as a steel rib structure covered first with polyurethane foam and then with an outer layer of polymer, creating a smooth, continuous surface.

1   Shape studies
2   Elevation

1_

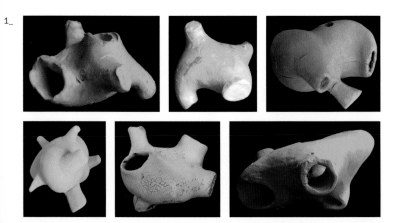

2_

3   Final shape study, rendering
4   Skeleton
5   Exit to the garden

3_

4_

5_

6_

   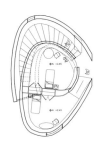

7_

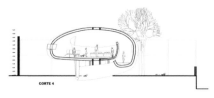 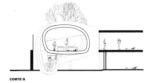

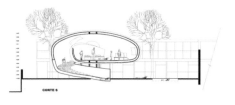 

8_

9_

WHITE SAND HOUSE

Guerrero, Mexico, 2001

This property is located on a private beach on the Pacific coast. The house was designed as vacation home where a large extended family could enjoy the beach and surrounding site. Local building codes require traditional houses with natural materials, such as stone, and a *palapa* (tropical thatch) or *tejado* (tiled) roof.

The concept is a single surface that becomes the edge between public and private. The public space is contained by a solid mass that holds services such as the kitchen, mudroom, and bathrooms. The private space is on the upper level, with five nearly identical bedrooms and three uniquely configured bathrooms.

1   Area schemes
2   Edge of main space

1_

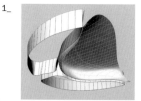 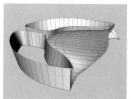 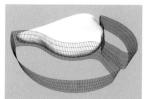

2_

3_

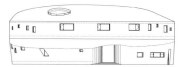 

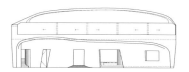 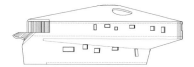

4_

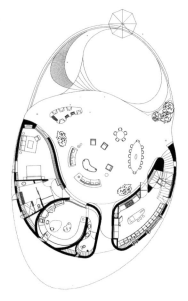 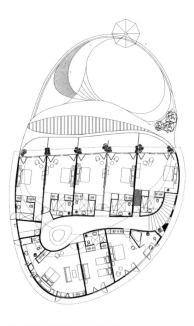

5_

6>

7_

8_

9_

10>

500-PERSON TOWER

Mexico City, 2003–05

The idea for this project was to make an organic building with a continuous skin facade. The shape is essentially a filleted diamond with rounded corners. The building is wrapped with louvers to introduce a sense of horizontality and movement to its vertical form.

The building is thirty-four stories tall and located in the fastest growing residential area in the city. It has various facilities for its residents, including conference rooms, saunas, a swimming pool, a gymnasium, and other recreational spaces. The tower sits atop a partly subterranean base, in which public areas and parking are located. There are 102 apartments, three per floor, at 1,700 square feet each. The total program is approximately 300,000 square feet on an 28,500 square-foot site. There are thirteen passenger elevators, a service elevator, and fire stairs.

1   Schemes
2   Rendering

1_

3_

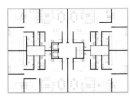 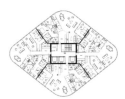 

4_

5>

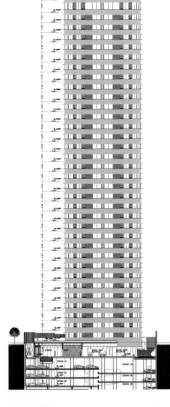 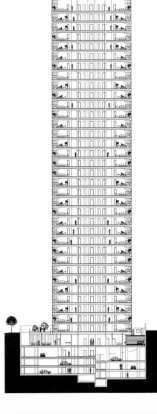

6_

GLASS FORTRESS

Mexico City, 2004

This tower is the result of new growth and life in the Mexican economy. Our
design is based on the translation of environmental and contextual relationships into built form through a series of manipulations performed on the building envelope. A high-rise, mixed-use building located on the edge of Chapultepec
Park, it combines offices, a hotel, and commercial space in a new "fortress"
and participates in the changing skyline of the city.

1   Proposed programs: offices, hotel, commerce
2   First compression
3   Second compression
4   Final compression
5   View with Chapultepec Park

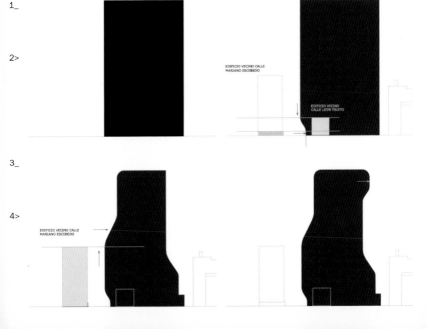

FILTERING TOY

Kanazawa, Japan, 2003–04

The Museum of the Twenty-first Century in Kanazawa commissioned us to design a landscape sculpture for their grounds. We decided to use the geometries of the existing museum building to produce a continuous, flexible structure in which children could play. The result is both transparent and opaque, independent and dependent, simple and dynamic, primitive and contemporary.

1   Concept diagrams
2   Tubular structure studies
3   Project on the site

1_

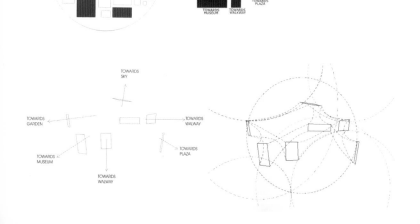

2_

3_

BRIDGING TEAHOUSE

Jing Dong, China, 2004

This is a commission for a small urban structure at Jinhua, Jing Dong. It floats on a pond, its shape a response to the surrounding landscape. Both the bridge and the teahouse are typical elements of Chinese gardens; this project is defined by the combination of the two. The Bridging Teahouse enables each user to experience his or her own ideal tea session in a unique, hybrid structure with five separate levels on which to sit.

1   Building studies of open structure

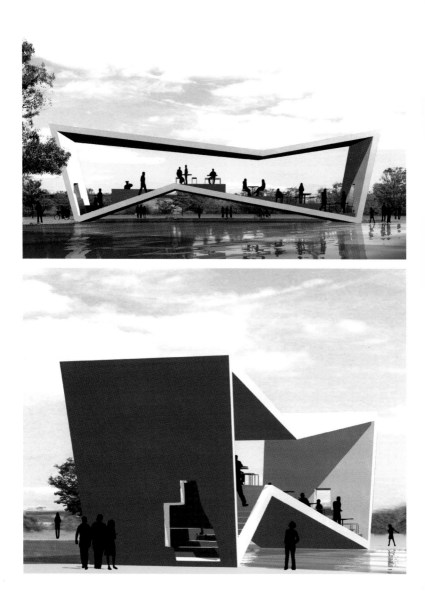

2   Perspective rendering

2_

EMERGENT

Founded in 1999 by Tom Wiscombe, EMERGENT is dedicated to researching issues of globalism, technology, and materiality through built form. Our work is concerned with the dissolution of critical practice and idealism in architecture in favor of locating and exploiting opportunities indigenous to a dynamic, networked society.

Our approach is informed by contemporary models of biology and business rather than by the arts. Ecologies and economies are evolutionary, interactive, and resilient—vital qualities that are conspicuously missing from architecture but necessary for survival in the postindustrial cultural landscape. We believe the future of architecture lies not in "never giving up" but in "giving in," seeking ways to leverage and incorporate differences. Our work therefore concentrates on the propagating logic of landscape, infrastructure, and network instead of the dead-end logic of order, vertical structure, and facade.

Recent projects have focused more on designing adaptive networks than on designing objects. Adaptive networks negotiate between multiple interests and territories. They create combined optimization rather than isolated optimization: structural, mechanical, and cladding systems are no longer understood as operatively discreet, but rather in terms of their ability to affiliate and feed back on one another to create value and beauty. The result is not deformational or dysfunctional, but co-evolutionary and synergetic. What the natural sciences have known for twenty years begins to inform our design approach, as architecture dissolves into what we like to call a "building science."

Most interesting to us is the phenomenon of *emergence*, which offers insight into the way isolated bodies, particles, or systems exhibit group behavior in consistent but unexpected patterns. The animated, vivid beauty of emergent organizations, such as in swarms or hives, is not merely a biological effect but potentially an environmental or atmospheric one. Buildings, instead of jumbled collections of idiosyncratic details or formal hierarchies, become integrated patterns or cellular arrays that exhibit behavior rather than simply contain space.

In a global economy where architectural design has become increasingly irrelevant—and indeed, often bypassed—we see adaptive, biological thinking as an imperative. We are therefore interested not just in applying these concepts to design methodology but also in investigating how they might transform the industry as a whole. This means developing co-operative relationships between architects, engineers, and fabricators, as well as developing new integrative methods of production, deployment, and construction.

1   Imagine a pack of wolves: the pack is beautiful because it is not merely a series of independent wolves, but also an emergent whole. When an opportunity arises, for instance the hunt, wolves spatially reorganize into the flexible, tactical array of the pack. This superorganism has the emergent properties of navigating as a liquid unit over varied topography and outmaneuvering its prey through multiple synchronized attacks. The pack is exponentially more resilient than the individual wolf, as it instinctively computes and leverages multiple spaces, speeds, and trajectories, into a synergistic, win-win enterprise.

2   The slime mold is an emergent organism, which opportunistically transforms its organization (from one to many) and behavior (from plant to animal) depending on environmental conditions. It is a Deleuzian "body without organs" par excellence.

3   Infrastructural networks and swarming systems converge into architectural organizations.
     (see also overleaf)

1_

2_

3>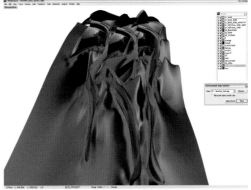

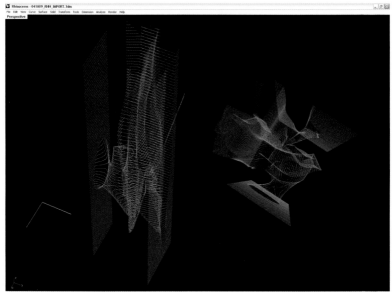

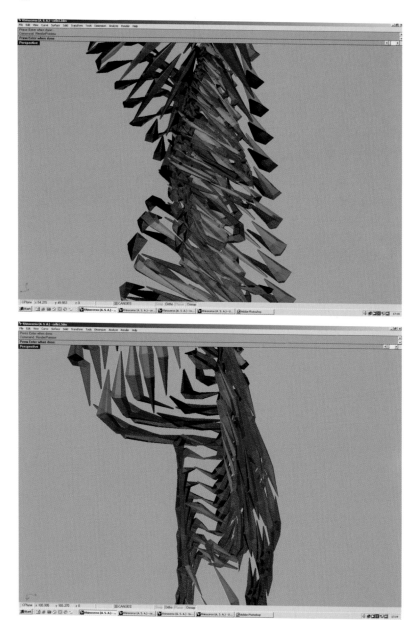

LAX COUNTERPROPOSAL 2015

Los Angeles, 1999

This design for the Los Angeles International Airport (LAX) extension is not an extension at all. Rather than enlarging the monolithic, axial body of the existing building (as planned by the city of L.A.), this counterproposal is distributive, creating a network of cells which proliferate opportunistically. There are at least seven airports, which is to say that there is a potential for a thousand micro-airports operating like a web of servers, sharing traffic volume, re-routing, negotiating times and trajectories. They do not operate independently, but in dynamic association.

This proposal is therefore more a software code than a master plan. The precise number, location, and size of each airport-cell would have to be recomputed as the urban landscape develops. Cells may be specialized to become hubs for cargo, international traffic, and business commuter traffic, each developing where they might best link into the city infrastructure and the runway system. Business partnerships in the airline industry, such as Star Alliance, could begin to self-organize into independently managed and controlled cells.

1_

2_

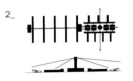 

1   Horizontal suburban terminals becoming urban terminal-towers
2   Linear development becoming cellular organization
3   Convergence of infrastructures in the International Cell
4   At least seven airports operating in a micromultiple network

3_

4_

PALOS VERDES ART CENTER

Los Angeles, 2000

This project began with the investigation of two key parts of the competition program—the sculpture garden and the lobby. Rather than relegating the sculpture garden to the back of the building and placing the lobby in the front in a kind of categorical arrangement, we decided to overlap their distinct behaviors in one space, creating an enclosed plaza with traits of both the natural and the urban. This space became the tissue connecting all of the other cultural functions of the building.

   In order to negotiate the open landscape and the discreet functions inside, we developed a flexible surface that could provide both global continuity and the potential for spatial nesting through local striations.

1_

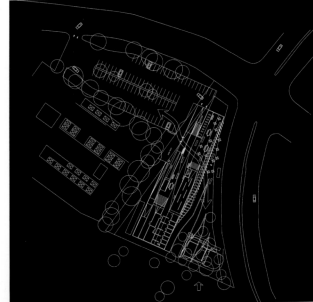

1   Site plan
2   North facade opening up to reveal an interior sculpture garden
3   Main entry from parking
4   Strips of terrain weaving into an architectural organization

2_

3_

4_

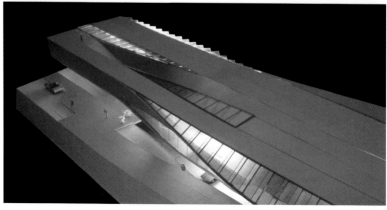

MICROMULTIPLE HOUSE

Los Angeles, 2001

This house is based on a mass-producible system implemented as an intercon-nected network of small, flexible bands. The bands are flat steel trusses, scaled to stack into standard delivery trucks and shipping containers—hence processes of construction and distribution are engineered into the system at the front end.

The bands operate according to simple rules, incorporating various behaviors and patterns of movement into their forms. Through topological bending and twisting, they conduct or arrest flows of bodies, vehicles, and light. Stairs, windows, and doors evolve performatively rather than being added syntactically.

The house emerges as a continuous living room, an effect of flexible, opportunistic processes and practices. Unlike Le Corbusier's famous "machine for living," this house is an abstract machinic organization.

1   X and Y vectors switch polarity to create twist in planes
2   Interconnected flexible units can become circulation, wall, or window
3   Continuity between house and landscape
4   Interior garden with nested spaces above

1_

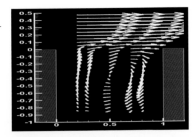

2_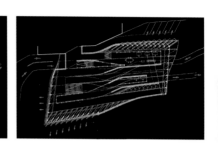

3_

4_

5   Ventrils to the north opening for natural ventilation

5_

RADIANT HYDRONIC HOUSE

Los Angeles, 2002–

This project is based on creating feedback between various building systems in order to break down the striated realms of technology and atmosphere. Rather than merely aestheticizing structural or mechanical engineering, the goal was to create spatial effects through switching and cross-fertilizing multiple structural and mechanical behaviors.

The house is organized around a hybrid spine/duct that integrates structural, mechanical, and circulatory functions into a single performative architectural device. Building systems are no longer conceptually exclusive and separately deployed, but synthesized into a fluid interior/exterior complex. The spine contains a reversible hydronic mechanical system that moves heated liquids from roof pools down to a radiant slab inside the house; it also transports cool westerly winds on summer evenings into a sub-floor to cool it for the following day. Ductwork in the spine opportunistically twists up to become structural supports in key locations and twists flat to become ramps and bridges. While each building system performs on its own, it does so only in relation to the others, functioning in a state of biological epistasis. No one system is optimized individually, but all systems are optimized in relation to one another.

The project is an interface connecting multiple disciplines; it is not just a design object but possibly the trace of a new way of practicing architecture.

1   In most contemporary architecture, structural and mechanical systems are designed in isolation, and then haphazardly collaged together. In the Radiant Hydronic House, as in the interplay between hyenas and lions on the African Savannah, these systems become interlaced in a kind of engineering ecology.

2   Network of parts adapting to become ductwork, ramps, and building envelope

1_

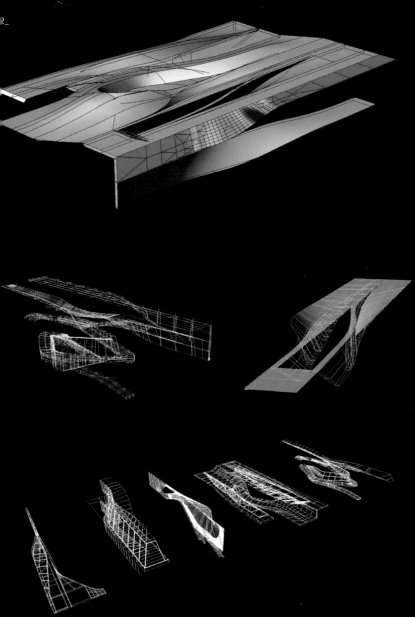

3   Development of snake-skin surfaces with single curvature
4   West elevation
5   Development of cellular pool structures
6   Duct/beam/stair/roof
7   Radiant hydronic system creates spatial ambience

3_

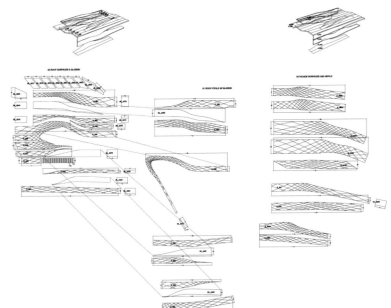

4_

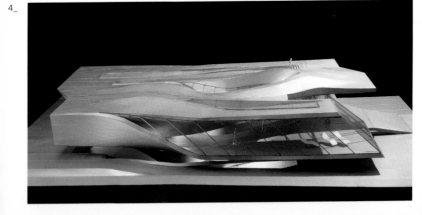

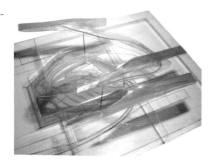

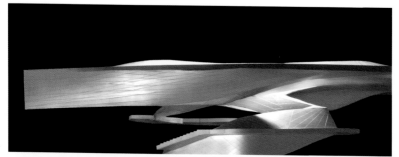

8_

9_

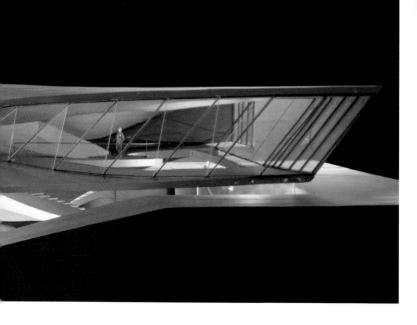

MOMA/P.S.1 URBAN BEACH

New York, 2003

Rather than attempting to collage representations of "beach" and "city," this project focuses on creating an atmosphere in which various combinations of behaviors, both recreational and cultural, can occur simultaneously.

The design is distinguished by two elements in a dynamic relationship—the Leisure Landscape and the Micromultiple Roof. The Leisure Landscape rhizomatically spills out into the P.S.1 courtyard, offering built-in furniture, sundecks for lounging, and three long lap pools for cooling off. Parts of this landscape adapt to become structural supports for the roof.

The Micromultiple Roof consists of a swarm of small, flexible units, or cells, which react locally to vertical and lateral forces and to sun-shading requirements. The interconnected cells work in alliance, enabling large, clear spans and forming a kind of structural ecology. At night, during the weekly DJ events, the roof transforms from a shade structure into a light-emitting body— a horizontal lantern stretching out into the city.

One of the driving goals of this project was to integrate issues of fabrication and erection into the design process. As a temporary event roof that had to be designed, manufactured, and installed in just two months, the project team was forced to jump directly from conceptual design to shop drawings—a feat made possible by computer modeling software. The key was to avoid designing a fixed shape and to concentrate on creating a system that could adapt seamlessly to changes in structural requirements, scope, and schedule. The cellular system of the Micromultiple Roof allowed for this flexibility, enabling us to fabricate in multiple locations and with multiple contractors simultaneously. All five hundred skin panels were generated algorithmically as single-curvature elements, making them easy to develop, water-jet cut, and transport. The project would not have been feasible or economical had we defined it with traditional construction documents rather than with adaptive geometry and computation.

Similar to cellular structures in nature, the structure of the P.S.1 Micromultiple Roof works based on the integrity of each individual cell working in association with neighboring cells.
Structural cells becoming light-emitting bodies at Warm-Up
View from above showing roof panelization

4   Ruled surfaces flattened for CAM water-jetting
5   Structural cells adapting to local moment forces and their location in the swarm
6   Crowd-density studies
7   Structural cells becoming light sources

4_

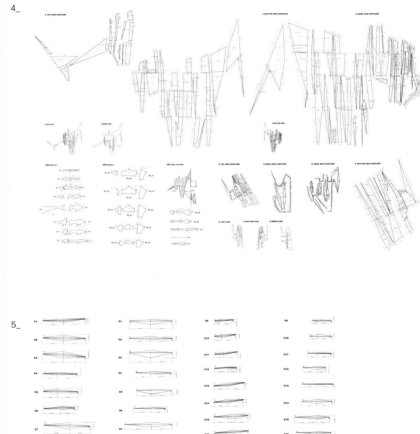

5_

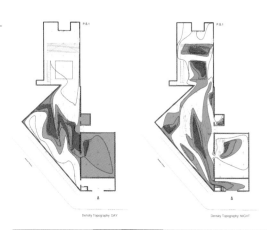

Density Topography: DAY

Density Topography: NIGHT

8   Rationalizing the curvature of the skin panels for fabrication
9   CNC milling studies
10   Structural cells organizing into an integrated long-span roof

8_

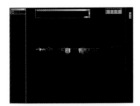

9>

10>

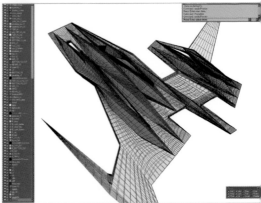

1   Outer skin becoming transparent
2   Plan
3   Warm-Up event: inhabiting the artificial landscape
    overleaf:
4   Crenelated skin wrapping structural cells

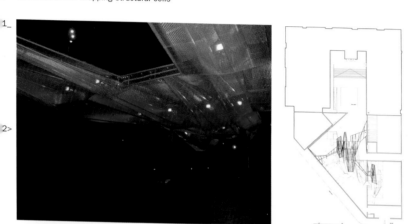

15_

STUDIO LUZ

We embrace our studio as a place for the study of an art; accordingly, each project we take on becomes a unique inquiry into architecture as a cultural expression. We find inspiration in popular culture, local craft, and abstraction, and believe that architecture is in a constant process of producing and reproducing social relationships. Through our work, we try to tap into these relationships in order to create something unexpected and refreshing. If architecture can establish a dialogic relationship with its users, receiving and creating meaning, then it can be a cultural expression affirming its relationship to the community in which it serves.

Studio Luz searches for opportunities within each project to promote interactivity, new modes of expression, and imaginative building techniques. Our works observe and react to various forms of cultural settings. They vary in scale of intervention, ranging from a mail slot, presented here, to a 13,000 square-foot Fellowship Center. Certain projects sponsor unique relationships between architecture, people, and technology. For example, as we have become immersed in the World Wide Web (a cultural symbol unto itself), we have proposed a mail-slot system that would serve as a network interface, search engine, visual display, and center for "real" mail distribution. In a lounge setting, we proposed using sensors and LED technology such that ambient lighting might react to the density of social activity, enhancing atmospheric mood. Other projects work through complex programs to provide social support by attracting diverse user groups. At any scale, architecture finds agency through identifying and re-inventing socio-ideological languages, thereby instigating change.

if...then: ARMATURE, INTERFACE, EXHIBITION

The Architectural League of New York
New York, 2004

Given the speculative context of the competition If...Then, our office took the opportunity to rethink and question our methods for the development of form, site, program, technology, and material. We became interested in creating an installation where the resultant architectural form is the culmination of actions and reactions. This was to be an experiment to explore and challenge our intuitions. Working within the logic of self-similar metal brackets and a set of spatial parameters, we sought to make a piece that was both a sculptural armature and interactive display. We conceived this framework to be dialogical in nature, from the process of construction to the required participation of the subjective viewer. The installation and the works presented within it observe, react to, and elicit responses from the users.

Project team: Michael Beaman

1   Digital model study
2   Digital sketch
3   Illuminated viewing devices
4   User interaction

1_

2>

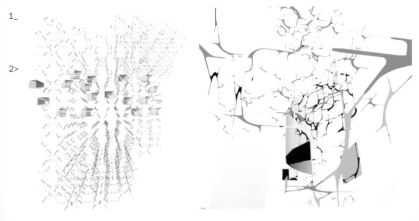

5_

6_

Armature elevation
User interaction
Conceptual sketches
Process
Stereoscope viewer

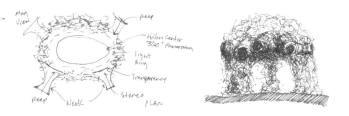

OMBAR

Boston, 2002

In the Ombar Lounge, VIP status is explored through the creation of privileged personal spaces, or display and repose. Occupying a former sub-street-level bank vault, Ombar is an exclusive dining room, lounge, and evening social club located in downtown Boston. The space retains existing features such as wrought iron bars and a twenty-five-ton vault door. The elite confine of the bank-vault-turned-lounge creates a new semi-public realm. Once inside, mood, exclusivity, and indulgence, as well as seduction and intimacy, are amplified.

The lounge is entered through a veil of white metallic ball-chain beads. This liner surrounds and shapes the space, creating an ambiguous relationship to the perimeter of the room with views to the DJ performance area and the entry stair. Projections are cast upon the beaded screen, providing a dynamic atmosphere of light and image, based on the desired setting. The design promotes a space that caters to an individual's subjective experience over traditional notions of mass consumption.

The floor and central column are comprised of a translucent combination of cement, resin, and an aggregate of recycled glass that creates a shifting array of niches for art as well as a source of deep ambient lighting. This material is poured in place on the floor and cast into panels to form the central column/light fixture.

1   Plan
2   Bar

1_

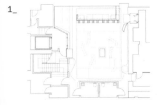

3_

4>

5>

6_

DIVA LOUNGE

Somerville, MA, 2004

The bubble-licious Diva Lounge is conceived as a gently wrapped haptic experience. The design investigates a responsive lighting system and atmosphere that register, change, entice, or accommodate a desired mood and react to the density of users. We propose an architectural skin that blushes: where groups of people gather, clouds of light form. Using low-voltage LED lighting, the Diva Lounge creates a metamorphosed yet intimate lounging environment.

A collection of architectural props populates the space and is used to elicit certain reactions. These elements are made of wormwood, a salvaged material from a disease-killed butternut forest in Vermont, each demonstrating various degrees of refinement. The pieces reconsider traditional subject/object relationships, becoming performance pieces that enable subtle means of communication or casual physical exchange. The curvilinear bench, for example, allows for clusters of people to sit together in a variety of arrangements, depending on the desired social setting.

The bathrooms are conceived as pods that respond to the ever-present bathroom line and recognize it as a significant social space in the lounge experience. Each bathroom has an illuminated top that glows dimly when occupied.

In a culture that is becoming more and more xenophobic, antiseptic barriers have increasingly mediated our tactile experiences. Within the lounge, patrons share various surfaces as a means of facilitating tactile physical exchange. The benches are made from soft, plump foam with wormwood backrests that allow passive, casual encounters. The design ambition is to use a combination of enticing materials and a sense of touch in order to promote intimacy.

The Diva Lounge project puts forth an architecture that makes observations about—and simultaneously creates opportunities for—casual social interactions. The space flirts with its users and in so doing amplifies the essence of a lounge experience.

Project team: Michael Beaman, Jason Frantzen

1   Lighting mockup
2   Entrance rendering

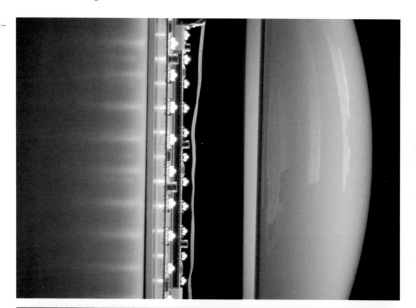

3_

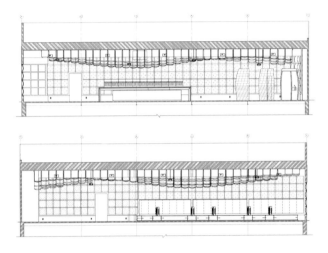

4_

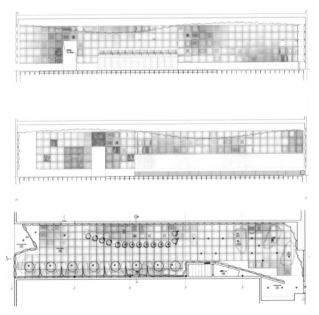

Sections and interior elevations
Interior elevations and RCP/cloud lighting effect
Plan details of log bar
Log at mill
Vermont butternut log bar
Bathroom plumbing pods
Floor plan

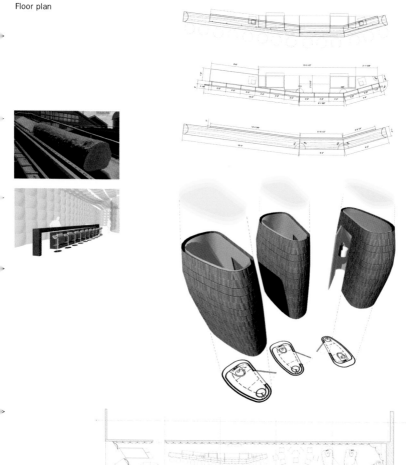

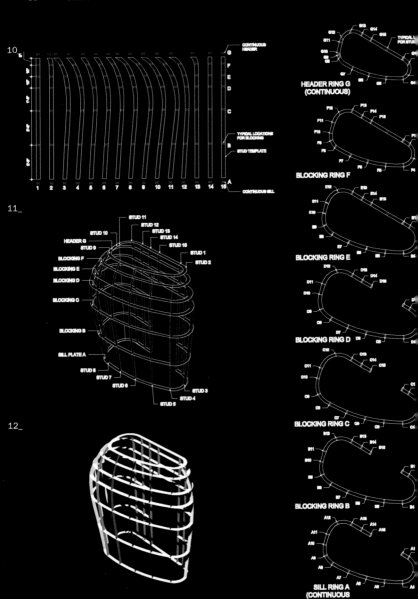

13_

14>

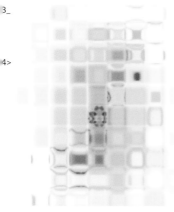

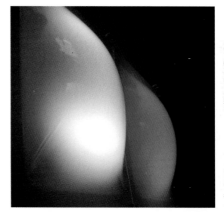

15_

W.O.W.: FACADE PROTOTYPES

Newton Highlands, MA, 2004

W.O.W. is an identity project for a women's clothing store. The store markets the work of local artisans, fabric painters, and clothing designers as an alternative to high-end boutique shops. The merchandise and image promoted by W.O.W. is eclectic and fun, demonstrating a healthy appreciation for craft and a sense of humor. Each new storefront seeks to capture this spirit and make a sensually constructed architectural artifact.

Pleated Prototype: Using the pleat as an architectural device, we proposed a fabric veil that would part and overlap various sections of the windows and entranceway. The pleats afford shaded glimpses of the interior displays and create a multilayered sunscreen for the southwest-facing facade. By investigating the use of various woven metal fabrics, their effects and fabrication techniques may be employed for other *pret-a-porter* facades. The Pleated Prototype alludes to notions of home sewing as well as the latest technologies for the developable surfaces needed for digital fabrication. The W.O.W. letters hang like tags on the back of a shirt—an overt touch of commercial kitsch. The result is a good-humored signage piece highlighting the nature of the retail venture it encloses and creating an occupiable expression of architecture.

Puzzle Prototype: More modest in appearance, this proposal creates a building visor that serves as sun-diffuser, display window, signage panel, and perimeter fence. The versatile cladding system employs notched polycarbonate sheets within irregularly shaped frames. The panels gang together to create the many different apertures for the display of goods and animate the facade with changing moiré patterns of reflected light. The panel system continues into the parking lot to enclose and define an entry courtyard.

Project team: Charles Austin, Jason Frantzen, Bukyung Kim

Elevations and plan
Model detail of pleats

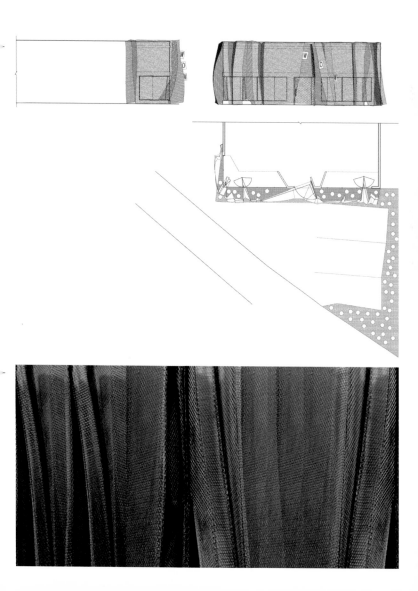

3_

4>

5_

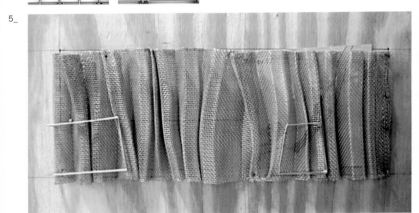

6_

Omega woven mesh
Sambesi woven mesh
Facade study model
Corner detail
Puzzle facade panels closed
Puzzle facade panels open

9_
10>
11>
12>

13_

14>

MAIL-SLOT SYSTEM

Harvard GSD, Architecture Department
Cambridge, MA, 1999

In the age of the Internet, the future of physical mail—and subsequently that of a formal mail distribution system—becomes increasingly questionable. The new symbols of cultural value are relational. This project examines the potential of a meta-structure, a machine that explores possibilities in the typology of the mailbox while serving as a traditional one.

As a physical matrix of the student body, the conventional mailbox system unfolds a unique and exciting moment: a moment of collectivity. The Mailslot System attempts to reinvent the typology by considering both its electronic nemesis and its important distinction as a physical collector. The system deploys two modes of interaction: a formal modality (a steel wall with approximately 320 mail slots) and a digital modality (a matrix of LEDs). It aims to become an important, vital element to the students—one that not merely receives but, transgressing a traditionally passive role, also transmits.

The project is fitted with a sixteen-by-twenty LED matrix (one LED for each receptor) linked to a terminal that is connected to the school database. This digital system can be assigned a number of uses, but ultimately remains endlessly reprogrammable. It can be used for purely pragmatic scenarios such as identifying a subset of mailboxes (a class, an interest group, a soccer team) or as a changing visual display. The computer interface allows a user to select the desired student group from the database, and once selected, the LEDs illuminate the corresponding mail slots. More sophisticated uses include notification for receipt of e-mail, real mail, or display of public messages. The applications of this expanded system as a locational and relational device are limitless.

The steel wall is formed and structured simultaneously. A digital template for a series of primary steel panels is pulled from a three-dimensional CAD model. The panels are bolted together at the flanges to construct a continuous three-dimensional face. This wall works as an integrated surface, in which the vertical and horizontal flanges provide structural integrity.

Project team: Michael Cosmas

"Plug-in" tray system

2   Typical mail slot
3   Mail slot, details
4   Elevation with illuminated fish pattern

5   View of wall intersection
6   Wireframe model
7   View from corridor

2_

3_
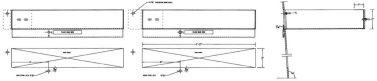

4_
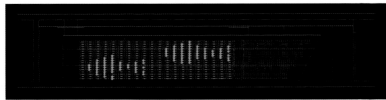

5_

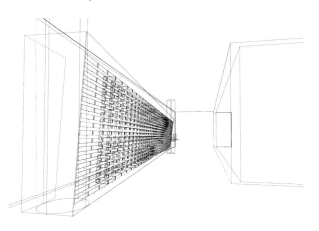

MITNICK RODDIER HICKS

It occurred to us that a "rereading of cities" could include challenging the long-standing authority of the city as the singular arena for the framing and legitimization of all cultural production. An effective rereading may have as much to do with the recalibration of centers and peripheries (including the myths and beliefs intrinsic to the desire for centers), and experimentation with other sources of orientation.

When asking ourselves how architecture might transform the urban experience, we also wondered how the awareness of eccentric sites, places, and events transforms our immediate sense of location, and furthermore, how a change in geographical focus might offset the cultural myopia inherent to the American lifestyle and the institutions that broker it.

Urban centers such as Manhattan, Los Angeles, Paris, and Tokyo have long stood as the hubs that determine, promote, and authenticate dominant forms of design production and dialog. Over the past thirty-five years, a new kind of architectural practice has emerged in which the sources for creative and institutional identity have been founded as much upon marginalized sites and contexts as upon more conspicuous discussions of the city.

If the leading model of cultural geography can be recalibrated to include overlooked sites, territories, and ideological demarcations, then new opportunities will appear for the re-inscription of urban, suburban, and rural contexts in terms other than those by which they have traditionally been defined.

Project geography

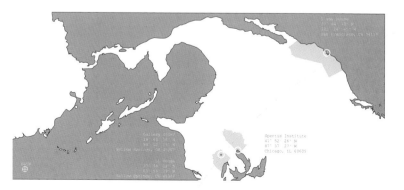

SPERTUS INSTITUTE

Chicago, 2002

Winner of the 2002 Burnham Prize Competition, this project proposes a new building for the Spertus Institute of Jewish Studies at its current location on Michigan Avenue, across from Grant Park and Lake Michigan. The competition called for a design that would engage ideas about institutional space, intersecting programs, and the representation of a consortium of culturally linked organizations within a single building. The program includes a library, museum, research center, and college. Additional themes involve the development of a strong civic presence along the monumental wall of existing buildings, and the promotion of greater interaction between the institution and the neighborhood.

As Jewish culture generally reflects a relatively placeless sensibility existing within the framework of other more geographically bound traditions, we became interested in the idea of the *dérive*, or the drifting of one set of activities across the spatial boundaries of another. The arrangement of program transgresses the grain of the more normative physical structure of the building, producing a pattern of relationships between form and program that is neither completely deviant nor overly conformist. Thus the registration of activity is never quite aligned with any fixed notion of spatial or programmatic autonomy; instead, different constellations of space and activity collide, intersect, and move across one another.

The main concept for the project was to form a collector of environments, institutions, programs, and people from the neighborhood. Groupings of activities would be transformed by unexpected intersections with other functions and spaces and would promote interaction between a diverse range of people. The non-institutionally specific elements, such as the gardens, entry plaza, and restaurants, are intended to attract students, museum visitors, and passersby to enjoy the place and take an interest in the various exhibits and activities housed in the Spertus Institute.

Books have the power to transform the way we see things both intellectually and perceptually, and written descriptions of events and places can sometimes be even more powerful and evocative than the actual things they portray. In a similar way, our experience of the built environment is as much the result of a collection of stories and interpretations as it is the consequence of direct visual experience. For this reason, the allusion to books as an emblem of reflection and learning and a repository for memory seems especially appropriate for a center for Jewish studies.

Symbolically, this project comes from the image of a varied collection of books arranged haphazardly in a series of offset rows and striations. The figure of the stacked rows of books and the voids between them suggests the history and diversity of the Jewish community. Like any group of individuals, the bookshelf exhibits an assortment of ages, colors, sizes, and varying degrees of wear and tear. Instead of making a building that monumentalizes a single resolute whole, we chose to explore a form that would engender disparity and difference within a spatially rich structure.

The form of the building was conceived as a collection of irregular volumes inserted across a stack of horizontal layers. Windows, apertures, and sectional overlays result from the arrangement of dissimilar spatial forms organized within a regularized frame. The figural primacy of the three main volumes, or voided inserts, remains in flux relative to the position of the viewer, causing perception to shift as one moves throughout the building.

Throughout the project the intention has been to bring the outside in and to reveal the interior to the exterior. The Institute is linked to the open area directly across Michigan Avenue through a ground-level passageway, a rooftop garden, and two green terraces located within the building envelope. The facade acts as a kind of screen that allows nature to peer out from behind a building that at times appears only as thick as the surface of its cladding, and at night, the green spaces—populated by day—are transformed into illuminated garden billboards.

Project team: Jon Stevens

1   Section diagram
2   Book collage with cityscape
3   Front photo-perspective

1_

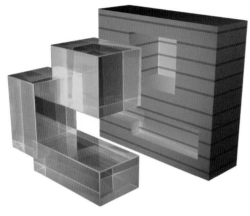

2_

5   Floor plans
6   Longitudinal section

5_

6_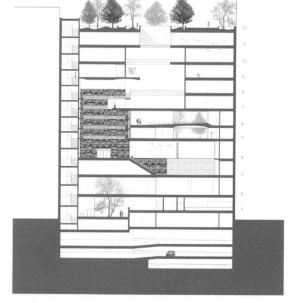

0_

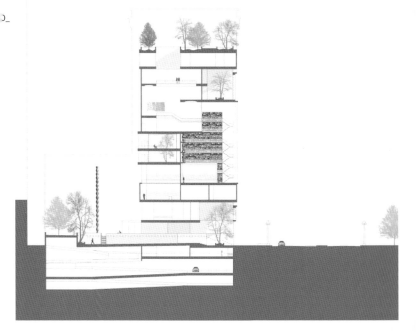

GALLERY 45387

Yellow Springs, OH, 2003

This project is a design for an art gallery in the small town of Yellow Springs, Ohio. The site is a 7,000-square-foot wedge-shaped parcel of land that sits between the campus of Antioch College and the Glen Helen Nature Preserve. The preserve is comprised of one thousand acres of forests, thickets, meadows, and rivers, and is host to about one hundred thousand visitors each year. Its geological features include valleys carved by glacial melt-water, ledges, cascades, and the yellow springs from which the town takes its name.

On one end of the site a pre-existing, flat-roofed structure is reconfigured to provide 2,000 square feet of interior exhibition space. An additional 5,000 square feet of outdoor area is provided for various events and the display of sculpture. The building straddles three distinct classifications of landscape: the forest, the picturesque park directly across the street, and the geometric form of the new sculpture yard.

Irregularly positioned infill walls respond to the rectilinear form of the block building by shaping the space into two distinct and outwardly thrusting figures. Three primary frames, comprised of the storefront, garden, and forest apertures, bind the two wedge-shaped volumes. The front facade alludes to the storefront windows of nearby commercial buildings and plays upon the image of the gallery as a storehouse of wares available for purchase. The camouflaged gray exterior allows the building to dissolve into an uninterrupted image of nature. The graphic form of the camouflage itself engages a twofold meditation on the optical mechanics of seeing, in this case invisibility and the rhetorical tendency of abstract imagery to signify dematerialization.

The sculpture yard is a geometrically determined and comparatively uniform field, while the interior building ground is an eccentric topography of sloping planes that tilt across thresholds of inside, outside, and the subsidiary territories within the building. From the submerged desk to the tilting lecture/presentation areas, the lack of registration between the ground and the enclosure challenges habituated assumptions about the role of the ground plane in the determination of space.

The gallery provides an unusual space for the presentation of art by collecting familiar forms in unexpected relationships. The building foregoes the conventional image of the white cube commonly associated with the display of art by combining it with storefronts, irregular ground planes, and picturesque window frames. It transforms a simple rectilinear box into a dynamic juncture of abstract forms with the particularities of its environment.

Site plan
Model
Floor plans

4_

5_

8_

9>

10_

Perspective view up ramp
View to sculpture yard
Reception area
Cross section
Perspective view from second floor

2-WAY HOUSE

San Francisco, 2002

The 2-Way House is located on the south side of Bernal Hill, a neighborhood in San Francisco that is rapidly transforming from a loosely arranged network of partially paved roads and randomly placed houses into a more uniform collection of large-scale homes. While most of the new houses in the area are bigger than any pre-existing structures, the client wished to build a home that was responsive to the scale of the extant building fabric, but without replicating prevalent material or stylistic typologies.

As the site is positioned just beneath the crest of a hill that hovers above the rest of the city, the building straddles two very different spatial scales: that of the narrow street and densely arranged houses above, and the extended views toward the Bay and cityscape below. The 2-Way House acts as a threshold across which these two scales merge, framing and promoting various aspects of this intersection.

The interior of the house consists of a network of smooth and continuous white planes devoid of materiality, while the kit-of-parts facade creates an image of the economy we have come to associate with prefab and modular construction, despite the fact that it is generally more expensive to reveal the structure than to conceal it.

By maintaining a clear distinction between the structural assembly on the outside and the more homogenized surfaces of the inside, the 2-Way House frames something of the traditional dichotomy by which interior and exterior have been distinguished—codes of materiality, construction, and patterns of habitation. In this case, the structure is apparent on the exterior, while inside the scale of interiority is transgressed through the diminishment of material difference and extended views of the city beyond.

Project team: Christopher Clinton, Wei Hu

Aerial map
Perspective from road

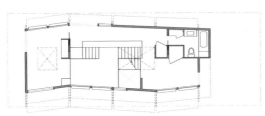

second floor plan

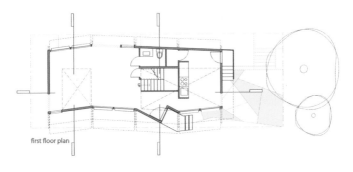

first floor plan

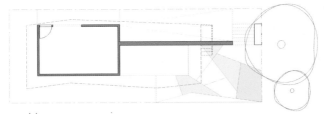

ground plan

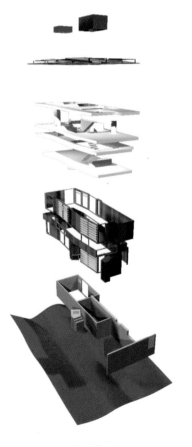

second floor + mid-level plans

first floor plan

6_
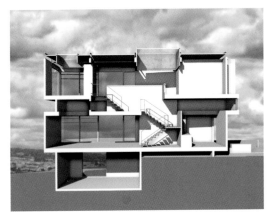

7_

Longitudinal section
View upstairs
Perspective view
View downstairs

LL HOUSE

Yellow Springs, OH, 2004–05

This is a design for a new 3,000-square-foot house in the remote college town of Yellow Springs, Ohio. Construction is to begin in the Fall of 2004. A small house currently sits on the site with a footprint of about seven hundred square feet. This building will be emptied of all interior structure and program to become an outdoor open area spatially engaged and serviceable to the new house. A large square aperture will be created in the roof of the existing house to bring light into the interior of the new home.

The form of the house plays upon the perceptual and symbolic relationships between inside and outside. Rather than create an extroverted public presence—or image—to the street, the house is inward-looking, and in many ways takes the experience of its own internal logic and inwardness as its subject.

The house is organized around three programmatic zones: a central multipurpose area, an elevated sleeping, bathing, and dressing zone, and a pair of lower-level guest rooms and bath. Without departing completely from the requirements and desires inherent to the traditional American home, the form of the house is intended to frame and challenge the long-standing model of the typical single-family home through visual transparency and rearrangements of customary material and territorial codes. The design of the LL House is intended to question how materiality may play into the structuring of views through the recoding of ordinary commercial and industrial materials in a domestic context, and how the rearrangement of spatial territories might serve to confound the conventional means by which architecture produces domesticity.

Project team: An Tai Lii, Dana Jaasund, Robert Schwartz

1_

Model
Diagram
Floor plans

1.   existing house
2.   entry
3.   office area
4.   main area
5.   wc
6.   pantry
7.   laundry
8.   mechanical
9.   exercise area
10.   auxiliary sleeping
11.   closet
12.   bedroom 1
13.   bathroom 1
14.   weather collector
15.   bedroom 2
16.   bedroom 3
17.   bathroom 2
18.   storage room
19.   coat storage
20.   linen closet

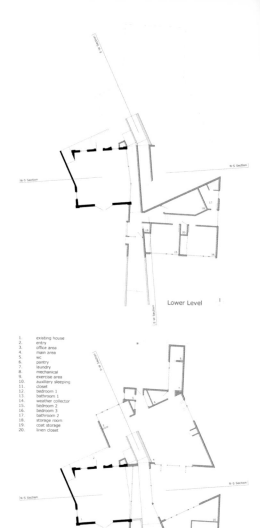

Lower Level

Ground Level

4   Site plan
5   Longitudinal section
6   Cross section

4_

7_

8>

9_

BORDEN PARTNERSHIP

Borden Partnership is an architecture, design, and research firm specializing in the advancement of affordable ultramodern design. Working with various materials, media, processes, and programs, our design strives to be a mediator of the everyday.

The conventional condition has the greatest potential for embodying culture; the suburban environment is our American average. The greatest need for design is in the everyday. Thus it is important that the types, economies, and material processes of our designs emerge from this condition. The architectural response must work toward the goal of synthesizing these systems to facilitate the production of cultural space that is both designed and obtainable.

The design process, driven by programmatic potentials and speculative reprogramming of the standard, demands cleverness and insight balanced by practicality and tectonics. Understanding the craft of making, overlaying a vision of living, embracing the common, and incessantly celebrating the inevitable will spawn an ultramodern architecture.

Standardization, prefabrication, seriality, and iconography become the primary building blocks in rethinking the conventional programs of living, working, and playing. The structuring of meaning in design, although articulated through form, program, material, cost, and context, is essentially linked through experience. This belief and the desire for its implementation in the everyday have led to the following projects.

Each project has been chosen to represent the effectual and practical potential of architecture as the fabricator of foundational spaces for cultural production. Each work emerges from a speculative fiction synthesized by experience.

VILLA HILDEGARD

Fluvanna, VA, 1998

Villa Hildegard is a typological residence that mediates the boundary between rural and urban. It is self-reliant and isolated yet connected to the city, riding an edge between the untamed wilderness and the controlled backdrop of the urban infrastructure. The result is a house that encompasses the economic and cultural sustenance of society and permits escapist and naturalist tendencies.

Designed for an individual, the house sits on a vacant site, unbuilt and open, surrounded by the wooded terrain at the foothills of the Blue Ridge Mountains and located on the banks of the James River. As the facilitating link to the city, the automobile serves as the foundation of the house. Responsible for its existence and primary in its organization, the vehicle bifurcates the house into public and private realms.

The plan articulates this tripartite construction of the house: private, automotive, and public. The guest wing houses two rooms, each with a court-yard and joined by a communal bathroom. The motor band is separated into an exterior court, which is a gravel garden contrasting with the surrounding wilder-ness, and an interior two-car garage. Finally, the main living quarters of the house exist in a single volume. An enormous double-height room is studded by three distinct elements suspended within. The amorphous forms of varying col-ors contain the bedroom, closet, and study. The living happens around the forms. A concrete perimeter wall defines the lower level. With the perimeter wall lined with books, the house provides insular protection from the realities of the world and an elevated platform upon which the individual can look back toward the city.

The model is a scaled manifestation of the villa. As a contained box it remains uncontaminated—sealed from the harshness of the world, isolated in ideal and setting.

Plan

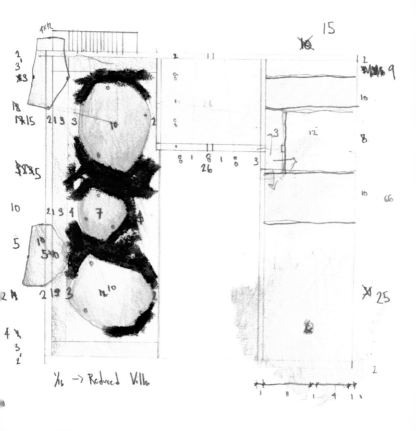

¹/₁₆ → Reduced Villa

2 Pod elevation studies
3 Aerial view toward entry, model
4 Pod-framing plans and elevations
5 First-floor plan
6 Second-floor plan
7 Roof plan
8 Section through front wall and pod

2>

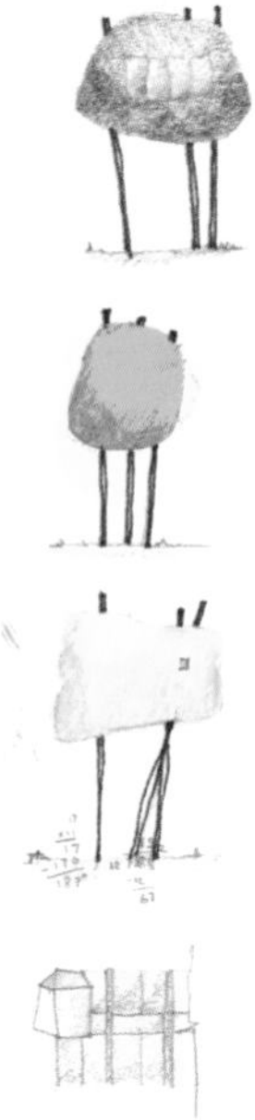

3_

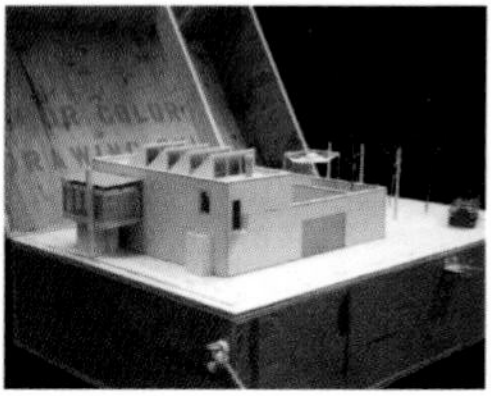

4_

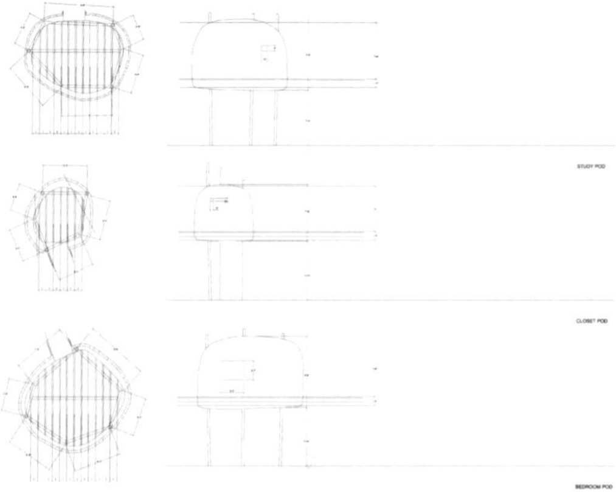

5>

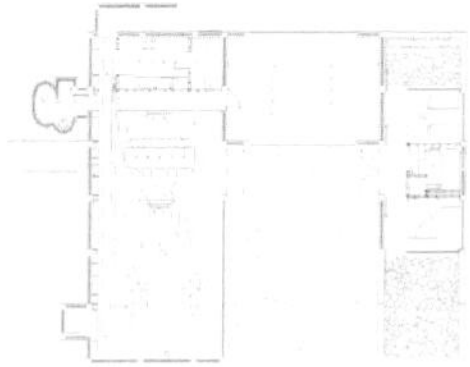

6>

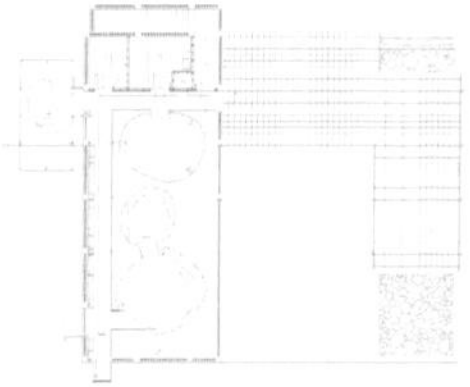

7>

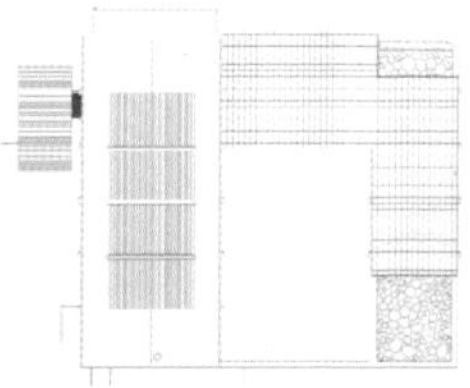

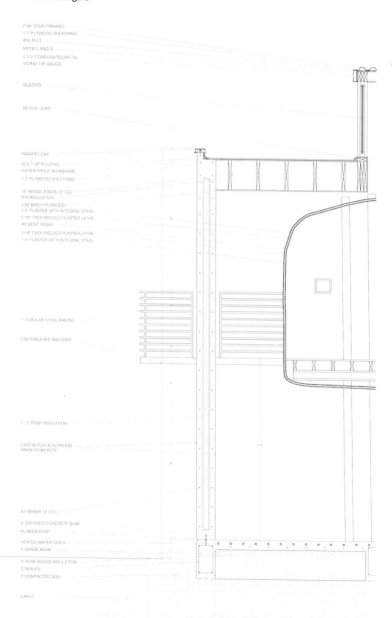

2"X6" STUD FRAMING
1/2" PLYWOOD SHEATHING
#30 FELT
METAL L ANGLE
2 1/2" CORRUGATED METAL
SIDING 1/8" GAUGE

GLAZING

REVEAL JOINT

PARAPET CAP
BUILT-UP ROOFING
WATER PROOF MEMBRANE
1/2" PLYWOOD SHEATHING

18" WOOD JOISTS 12" O.C
R14 INSULATION
4'X8' BIRCH PLYWOOD
1/4" PLASTER WITH INTEGRAL STAIN
1/16" TACK WELDED PLASTER LATHE
#3 BENT REBAR
1/16" TACK WELDED PLASTER LATHE
1/4" PLASTER WITH INTEGRAL STAIN

1" TUBULAR STEEL RAILING

CANTILEVERED BALCONY

2 - 2" RIGID INSULATION

CAST IN PLACE PLYWOOD
FINISH CONCRETE

#4 REBAR 12" O.C.

6" EXPOSED CONCRETE SLAB
RUBBER STOP

HEATED WATER COILS
2' GRADE BEAM

4" RIGID BOARD INSULATION
STIRRUPS
2' COMPACTED SOIL

EARTH

NON-CONSUMPTIVE SPACES

Tokyo, 2001

Civic space is ingrained in the infrastructural mapping of the city plan. The in-between spaces that are the voids of the city are prime with potential for the insertion of public areas. The architectural event must be a non-consumptive facilitator providing a free, public-instigating experience. The solution is an infrastructure of seven truly public spaces. The site is on the edge of the techno-city Tokyo, representative of any and all cities. A network of pavilions, each remaining distinct, come together through the event.

Allotment Gardens: By reinserting a natural condition into the constructed landscape of urbanity, the garden serves as a ground of congregation and recreation. The field is stripped with varying prismatic colors, densities, and heights. A small pavilion acts as a tool shed.

Public Restroom Facilities: The bathroom pavilion is a double blur. The outer shell of opaque glass spirally cloaks two interior unisex facilities. The field surrounding the pavilion consists of a group of shallow reflecting pools of varying temperatures that also serve as fountainhead showers.

Library: The library pavilion is dispersed across the landscape, a direct contradiction to the introverted process of collecting information. Three glass folds act as a canopy that defines place amidst the field of poles. A catalog of books dangles as a loose hypostyle hall of corded classics.

Image Screens: A series of computer stations command digital billboards, exposing the accessed imagery to the city. The field becomes a projected realm of changing information. Randomized imagery undulates across the surfaces when the interface is vacant.

Disco: A mobile discotheque formulates an event through an audible infrastructure. A glass cage containing the sound system and mixing tables allows the event to begin at the instigation of the DJ. The operable perimeter walls unfold to form a stage and reveal the interior equipment.

Allotment gardens, tool shed
Public restroom, aerial view
Library, canopy with seating
Image screens, information billboard field
Disco, open

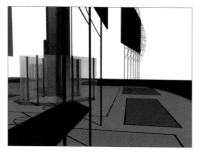

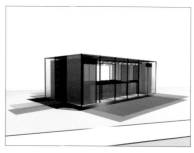

PEDESTRIAN BRIDGE

Seaside, FL, 2001

A gateway constructed at the western edge of Seaside, Florida, marks the threshold of a unique community. A pedestrian bridge spanning Highway 30-A, the primary approach to Seaside, becomes a viewing machine to provide vistas, isolated vantages, and highlights of the city and its architectural identity. An open competition called for a ceremonial landmark to commemorate the twentieth anniversary of Seaside; the monument, which serves as gate, frame, filter, lens, and bridge, reflects the community's established traditions and crosses its past with its future. This design was a response to the legacy and attitudes represented by Seaside and ultimately by New Urbanism. The structure serves simultaneously as a celebration and a critique.

Constructed of heavy timber and sheathed in a wood lattice, the striated face maintains transparency through the gateway and across the horizon. The same lattice system wraps the roof plane, allowing the crisp light and transitional weather to penetrate the structure. Each end is capped by a helical stair that encircles a grid of two-story steel wind chimes. A single detached tower provides an elevated viewing platform. The deck itself, while becoming a corridor for traversing the ever-increasing tourist automobile traffic, has moments of pause with windows facing Seaside. The opposite face has a linear band window that uniformly blankets the highway lanes extending to the horizon and the adjacent sprawl.

The pavilion serves as a frame: a literal provider of specific vantages isolating distinct moments and chronologically gathering the history, development, and collected urban vision that defines Seaside.

1_

2>

Underbelly
Continuous highway face, view toward east
Second-floor plan
Worm's-eye view
View funnels piercing through lattice cladding
Continuous ribbon window
Viewing chamber

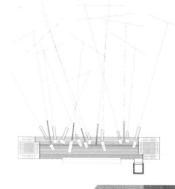

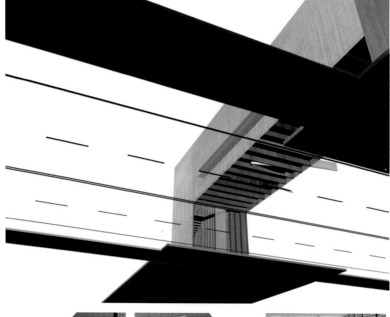

RUBBER-BANDED HOUSE

Raleigh, NC, 2002

The form of the house defines the identity of the domestic realm. Its activities are governed by the spaces in which they are orchestrated. Positioning the single-family home in a postwar suburb allowed for an investigation of the domestic landscape. Split between public and private, the house is a double helix: two interlocked loops, each belonging to different social spheres. Their adjacency creates a dialogue between the two realms.

The private space is represented as a solid ring, wrapped in birch plywood. The patterned skin of the facade cracks back at distinct moments to form apertures. In section, the ends of the second-story volume become vertical circulation spaces and the upper deck establishes a private living area, while the subterranean level below provides protected areas for sleeping and bathing. The public space, which lies in between the private sectors, is perpetually traversed.

This between space is both an interior and exterior condition. The traditional yard becomes public, including a patio for grilling, an auto court, and a garden with a field of grass and a wall of trees. The inner public space is a continuous loop encompassed by a single rubber wall. Constructed out of a series of operable vertical structural poles and a flexible membrane of traditional rubber bands, the wall undulates as it reacts to the inhabitants. As a screen, the rubber-banded wall modulates light and provides for a flexible layout through its tactile latticed surface.

1_

2>

3>

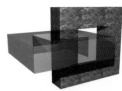

Rubber bands
Rubber lattice wall, detail
Public (open) and private (closed) links
View from street
Full-scale mutable wall detail

6_

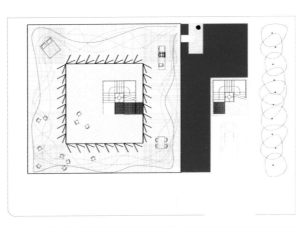

7_

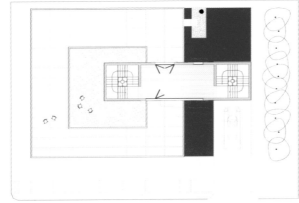

8_

9>

First-floor plan, public living
Second-floor plan, private living
View through rubber wall
View along rubber wall
X-ray view along street
Rubber-banded wall configuration

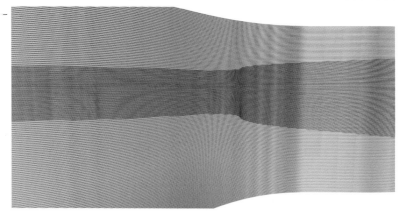

6 OF 20

Propositions for Suburban Living, 2003

The following propositions introduce ultramodern single-family housing into the contemporary landscape. Twenty houses have been developed, of which six are illustrated here in greater detail. The houses employ modularity, program, materials, light, culture, and careful spatial planning to maintain affordability, update design, and increase the quality of the space and composition. These proposals represent aspects of the current suburban domestic condition but suggest a new way of living. They attempt to make the ordinary extraordinary.

The current single-family house subscribes to a model that addresses bank loan guidelines but denies the contemporary cultural condition. The forms, functions, and styles, though commonplace, are anachronistic and divorced from their original intention. The focus on type, via technology rather than nostalgia, provides meaning through formal, functional, and cultural evolution. The following propositions present opportunities for the conventional and average condition—a reconsideration of the single-family home. Iterations based upon the standard economic, programmatic, and functional needs illustrate the potential to find architecture in the ordinary. By focusing on both the process and the fabrication of the house, the prototypes suggest a method of design that positions contemporary culture as the foundation for specific and viable solutions for changing our constructed landscape.

The Program House relies upon three guiding principles: the articulation of form based upon program, the collection of programs in an indoor-outdoor plinth, and the ability to phase these programs over time. Their collection results in an interstitial space that bridges and blurs the boundary and compartmentalization of both program and house.

The Gradient House delineates program between public and private functions into two identical bars. Shifted geometries allow for the two bars to overlap and create a diversity of residual spaces throughout the site. The floor plates slide past each of the boxes to provide a substantial rear porch.

The Porch House links the landscape and the daily activities of the house. Despite the small and confined lot, an exterior room is carved out of the multiple programmatic pavilions that make up the house.

The Tube House organizes daily domestic activities into a linear, twenty-four-hour cul-de-sac of spatial activity. The cycle advances and reverses relative to the use of each space, including the garage, entry, kitchen, dining room, living room, utility room, stairway, closet, bathroom, and bedroom.

The Constellation House shifts the traditional wall openings to the roof. The large roof apertures draw light deep into the house, articulating each space and its function based upon varying densities of light. This gradation allows for efficiently scaled areas that change spatial qualities dramatically over time.

The Enclosure House relies on a single wrapper of standing-seam metal to enclose itself. Recessed end walls, which provide both front and back porches, establish a front public face with functionally choreographed, punched openings, while the back wall is a transparent, operable facade incrementally studded with color metal panels for storage. The central core contains the functional service components, bifurcating the house into public and private realms.

Program House: programmatic zones
Gradient House: prefabricated unit shift
Porch House: phasing
Tube House: live, circulate, sleep
Constellation House: roof light-funnels
Enclosure House: elements

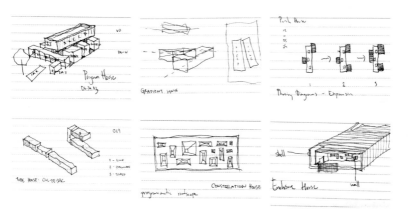

1   Program House plan
2   Aerial view
3   Longitudinal section
4   View across living field

1>

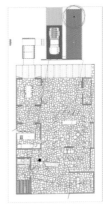

2_

3>

4_

Gradient House plan
View from back yard
Transverse section
View of rear porch

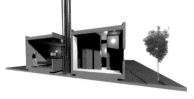

1   Porch House plan
2   Living pavilion
3   Longitudinal section, private bar
4   View from living pavilion across porch

1>

2_

3>

4_

Tube House plan
Rear view
Longitudinal section
View from living space

1   Constellation House plan
2   Aerial rear view
3   Longitudinal section
4   View of public living space

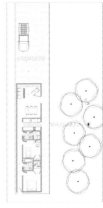

1>

2_

3>

4_

Enclosure House plan
View from street
Longitudinal section
View of front public living space

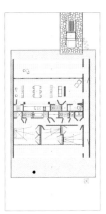

ARCHITECTURAL MECHANISMS

(X)perience Pavilions, 2004

Each carefully positioned pavilion represents a distinct experience. The spaces are articulated for watching, reclining, residing, entering, moving, and engaging place. Twenty-four mechanisms have been developed, four of which are highlighted here.

3 Box: Three cubes placed in sequence define the volume of the 3 Box pavilion. Two columnar structures, one made up of an ordered nine-square grid and the other of three disordered sculptural pins, elevate the inhabitable plane. The variation from light to dark, achieved through the alternating open and closed facade, provides for a private sleeping platform.

Aperture Box: The perforated shell, with a large array of openings, transforms the building into a viewing chamber. The windows, articulated through precise cuts, thin slices, elongated punctures, and tiny piercings, mediate between formal frame, ambient light portal, and ventilation system. The grand hall serves as a communal living room flooded with fragmented images of the surrounding landscape.

Light Tube: A corridor of light is formed by diverse roof apertures and alternating horizontal windows. The linear path moves through varied light densities and views. A long central table serves as the communal dining hall.

Up Down House: Two iconic images of the home are perforated with diverse apertures and are flipped relative to one another. Their form and skin challenge conventional perception. Each serves as a residential unit.

1_

2>

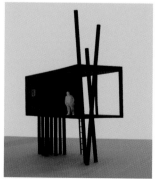
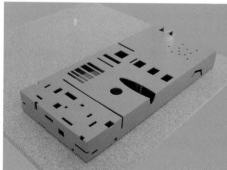

3 Box, model
Aperture Box, model
3 Box, plan and elevation
Aperture Box, plan and diagrams

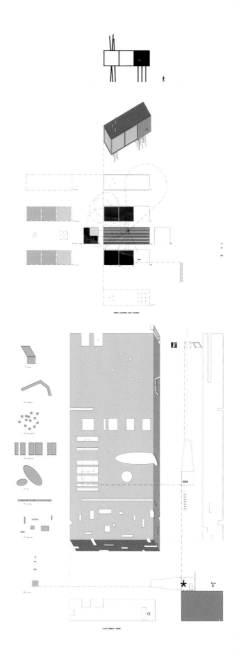

5   Light Tube, axonometric and diagrams
6   Light Tube, model

5_

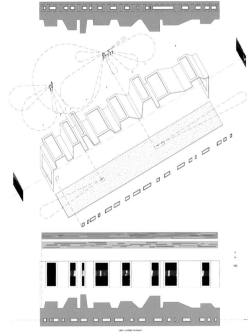

6_

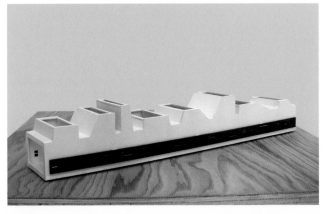

Up Down House, axonometric and diagrams
Up Down House, model

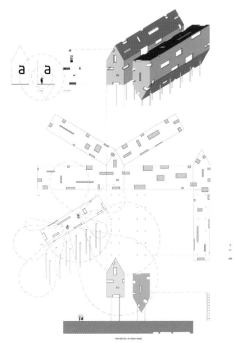

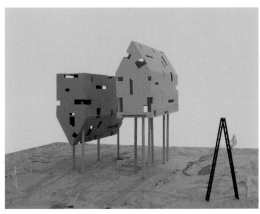

MILOBY IDEASYSTEM

Miloby Ideasystem began as an experiment by two architects looking to fuse their approach in architecture to other media. The ambition was to create a working environment that did not make architecture *à la carte* but as a mutable creative strategy, a system, that informs the materialization process indifferent to scale, discipline, or media. We wanted to test the role of architects and develop a vehicle for intuition, theory, and pop culture to influence the context in which design is considered—from strategy, development, and production to brand identity, advertising, and the built environment.

However itinerant the path of a specific project, our approach has two characteristic cycles, one reductive and the other additive: 1. Distillation. Through research and analysis we distill the context of a project, its unique circumstance and/or narrative, into a theoretical model—a model that exploits some other richer and more familiar system in order to describe the subject being investigated. 2. Translation. Inherently a theoretical model holds conceptual relations that are not part of the original analogy—the surplus meaning, or open texture. As these new relations between the model and the subject are identified we begin to translate them into material, digital, or written parts as a method of discovery. The ambition of installing an external apparatus, a conceptual modeling tool, is to challenge our own predetermined notions and reflex actions while providing a means of ordering the investigative process.

Miloby Ideasystem remains a venture in conjugating contemporary design discourse with clients, budgets, and technology. The plan is to continue to speculate, test, and make things under the influence of the world that surrounds them.

MOTOR LODGE

New York, 2002

This project was commissioned by a developer interested in the urban motel as a counterpoint to the wave of boutique hotel construction in Manhattan. Sited in the art gallery district of West Chelsea, the design uses the neighborhood's urban industrial typology to reinterpret the ubiquitous courtyard hotel.

    Like the vertical car-storage structures of local parking lots, the rooms of this hotel are individual pods stacked in an open steel frame and wrapped with a glass skin to reveal levels of occupancy. Loyal to the motel experience, the design has no interior corridors and provides direct access to rooms from exterior circulation. The design works to displace the typical street-level boutique hotel scene into the vertical space of the interior courtyard by opening it to the sky and centering a nightclub at its base.

1_

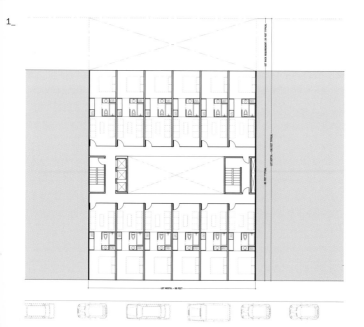

Typical plan
Concept
Courtyard elevation showing stacked motel rooms
View from street
Street elevation

2W45

New York, 2003

We received the commission to rebrand one of New York's foremost post-production studios—Charlex. From the logo and website to print ads, we revamped the company's look and feel. Charlex realized that for their clients to recognize progress they needed to experience it in their built environment; architecture needed to be part of the new brand identity.

      The 12,000-square-foot office project involved the reorganization of fifteen edit studios, a sophisticated data/com network, and a circulation hierarchy allowing competing accounts to work furtively. Since Charlex operates much like a hotel, it was conceived as a main branded volume into which individual edit/fx studios are inserted and treated as brand-neutral. The main volume, housing shared services and lounge areas, was designed as a continuous plywood surface acting as a spine between the two floors, moving traffic and digital information between studios, the centralized server room, and support offices. Awareness of passing from the studio onto the branded volume, from Charlex areas to client areas, is heightened by misalignments of thresholds and exposed edges.

1>

2_

Charlex branding project
Logo
Diagram of plywood spine

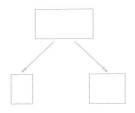

4X8 UNIT **MATERIAL**

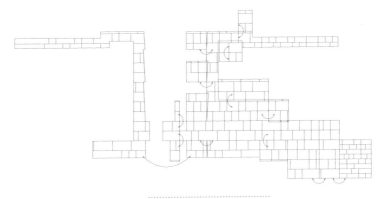

PROGRAMMED **SURFACE**

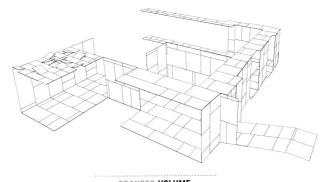

BRANDED **VOLUME**

4_

5>

6_
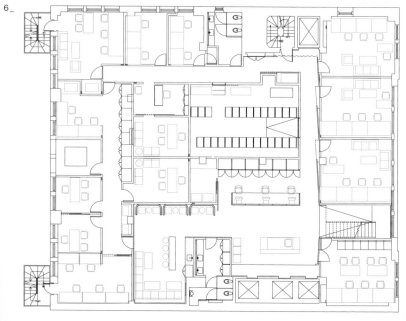

Corridor looking west
Corridor looking east
Plan
Pixelated ceiling at brasserie
Reception
Edge condition of plywood spine at lobby

LUCINI ITALIA EXECUTIVE OFFICES

Miami, 2004

When national gourmet brand Lucini Italia relocated to Miami, they wanted their new executive offices to be a brand experience, reflect their progressive business approach, and inspire creativity in the people who work there. Above all, Lucini Italia wanted visual access to the spectacular views of the Atlantic Ocean and the Miami skyline. This project was awarded a Solutia International Design Award for its innovative use of glass in 2004.

The conceptual gesture was to celebrate the brand via its flagship product—extra virgin olive oil. Rather than sentimentalizing the Italian experience, the project relied on strong distillation and a bold material palette for its contemporary translation of the Lucini Italia brand. Luminous green glass panels and contrasting thick dark walls (bulkheads) create a series of framed views of the water and skyline. The bulkheads house the custom workstations, storage, and office equipment, while the frameless moveable glass partitions blur the delineation between private office and corridor.

With a limited budget, every possible element needed to buttress the core narrative. A conventional Armstrong dropped ceiling was installed with custom transparent polycarbonate panels to transform the surface into a giant diffuse lightbox. Slits in the ceiling, from which the green laminated glass partitions are hung, double as return-air openings. The product-sample storage was exposed to become a graphic element, and the conference room table design was conceived as an overgrown dining table to be used for product-tasting events.

1_

Lucini Italia extra virgin olive oil
Diagrams
Offices looking north

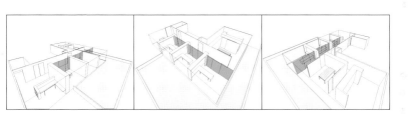

4_

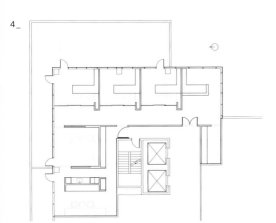

5_

Plan
Detail of sliding-glass partition at ceiling
Offices looking south
Reception

MUNROE COTTAGES

Miami, 2004

Morphing from simple wood-frame beach cottages of the 1920s to miniature Spanish-inspired villas, these two small structures survived over eighty years of style abuse. Now stranded within a gated community of luxury homes, the property was sold with heavy deed restrictions and an architectural control committee in an attempt to preserve their historic value. The cottages could not be torn down, their street elevations could not be altered, and any new construction was limited to a twelve-by-twenty-foot area directly behind them. Our task was to modernize and merge the two separate structures into one larger home.

By conceptually wedging the structures together from the rear and leaving behind an absent form, we unified, reordered, and reoriented the home. The removal of this conceptual disruption exposed the interior spaces of the cottages to sunlight and a lush backyard. The interior portion of this wedge is the center of the new plan, containing the kitchen and study. Extending outside into the landscape, the wedge is defined by a private terrace, bamboo walls, and a metal carport.

1_

2_

Wedge study models
Concept diagram
Study models

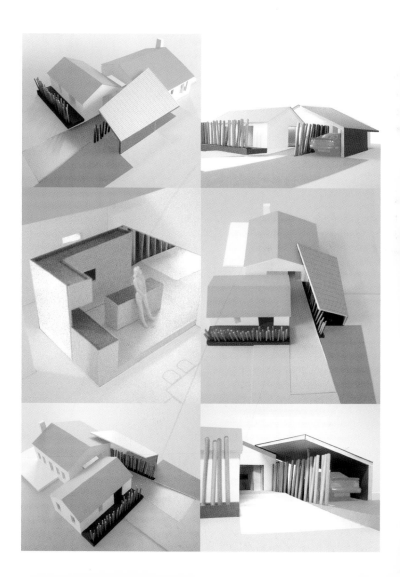

4>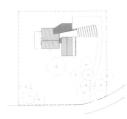

5_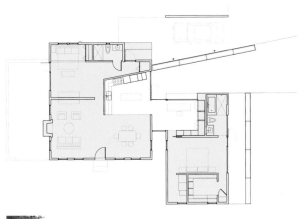

6_

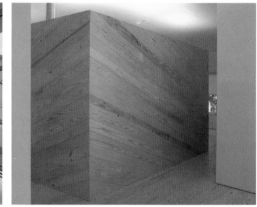

SANTA FE HOUSE

Santa Fe, 2001

This project was commissioned by a newly divorced woman who relocated from her exclusive Chicago neighborhood to the wilds of New Mexico. High in the mountains outside of Santa Fe, as far as she dared to drive her SUV, our client purchased a piece of land to build her new life. Like others who head west, she wanted to retain traces of her past—the modern architecture she left in Chicago and the red barns from her youth in Connecticut. We recognized that the real project was the introspective exploration of cognitive place; the personal expression of context.

The ambiguity between her desire for cloisterlike solitude and love of the expansive views precipitated two complimentary parts—the skin and the viewfinder—manifest in the red-painted cedar siding and elevated platform. The design is a hybrid using qualities of both the Miesian glass house and the vernacular barn.

The ground floor consists of a viewing platform that rises as it extends across the steep slope of the site. As it lifts, it opens to the surrounding views and landscape, and helps protect against the local bear population. The red-painted wood skin wraps the platform to create interior living spaces. At the second floor the skin wraps more tightly, providing the small and hidden spaces the client desired for writing and sleeping.

1_

2>

Concept diagram
View from access road
View downhill
Looking toward outdoor viewing platform
View from platform

MARINE MUSEUM COMPETITION

Aland, 2003

Located in the Baltic Sea between Finland and Sweden, this small island nation of Aland was once a world-class shipping power and renowned for its historic fleet of windjammers. In 2003 Aland issued a competition brief for an extension to their national marine museum as part of an economic revitalization plan. This design is our submission to the competition.

　　Our design is a formal contemplation of the future of Aland told through its history with the sea—the story of a country of the sea housed in a building of the sea. The project is a decisive move away from the romantic historicism and sentimental objectification typical of other Aland revitalization efforts. Like the cold black water of the Baltic, the building crashes onto the shore to weave together sailing's codifications of the sea—its geometry, anatomy, and disrupted horizons.

1_

Concept diagram
Site plan

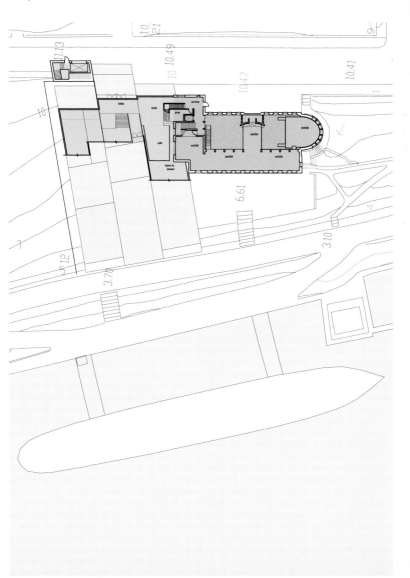

3_

4>

5_

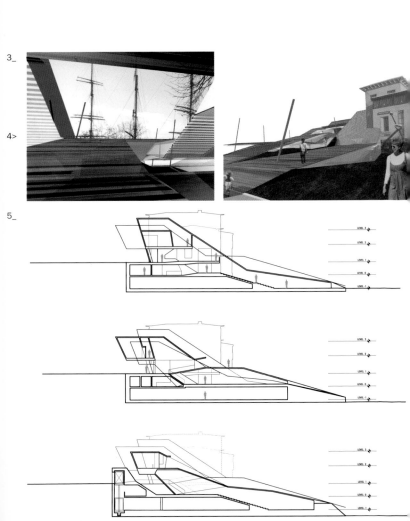

28BL

East Hampton, NY, 2004

Our client purchased a poorly conceived and partially completed house on his favorite street in East Hampton. Abandoned by a developer who had hoped to make a quick profit, the original house sat unfinished on a thin, one-acre lot. Our job was to convert the Home Depot Cape Cod into a modern home worthy of its Beach Lane address.

To bring a needed sense of formal clarity we applied a series of blunt and rational moves:

Step one: clean. We cut off, cut out, flattened, or filled anything extraneous.

Step two: mirror. To accommodate additional program we mirrored the north wing.

Step three: shear. To comply with zoning setback regulations we sheared the new wing.

Step four: open and close. To foster outdoor summer living we cut open the ground floor; for the winter season, we layered it with scrims.

Step five: connect. To engage the extra-long landscape we blurred the transition from interior to exterior with a landscaped plinth.

1_

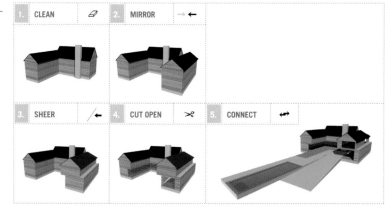

4_

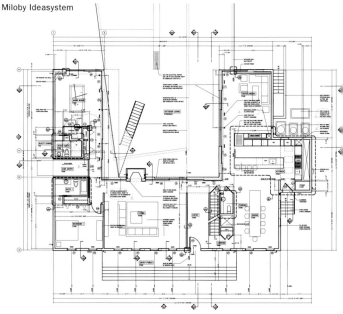

5_

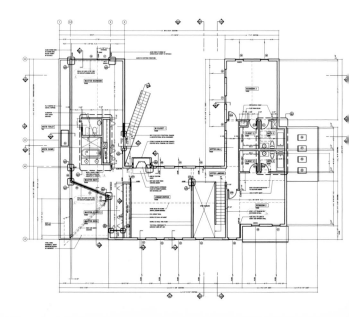

Ground-floor plan
Second-floor plan
Construction
View from inside, doors open
View from inside, doors closed

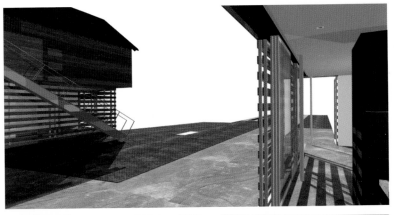

...then